Glasgow Locomotive Builder to Britain

Glasgow Locomotive Builder to Britain

Murdoch Nicolson

Hyde Park Works and Atlas Works in the 1950s.

Acknowledgements

The author would like to thank the following for assistance in the preparation of this book: Mr Andrew Jackson, Libraries and Archives, for editing the text; Mr Don Martin, East Dumbartonshire Libraries, for his assistance and advice concerning the Murdoch & Aitken Locomotives; the ladies of Libraries and Archives typing pool for transcribing the text and the staff of the Photographic and Graphic Departments, especially Margaret Thomson for design and layout of the book.

All illustrations, unless otherwise stated, have come from the North British Locomotive Company and constituent material housed in the Mitchell Library, Glasgow.

Cover photograph: Caledonian Railway "Royal Pilot" No. 123

Published by Glasgow City Libraries and Archives
© 1998

ISBN 0 906169 53 4
Printed by Cordfall Ltd

Libraries and Archives

Introduction

Glasgow has been synonymous with heavy engineering, especially shipbuilding, since the early nineteenth century. One important branch of this industry, whose products were only slightly less impressive than the great ships which slid off the Clyde slipways, was the construction of railway locomotives. As the Empire expanded and Britain became increasingly industrialised, a need developed for the transportation of passengers and goods from coast to coast, from north to south, from east to west, and from all points in between. This transport growth occurred in every continent across the world. As railway networks spread, first over Britain, then throughout other countries, production demand increased. The production of locomotives in Glasgow increased with the demand; from the first steam locomotive in the city, to the establishment in 1903 of what was to be the third largest locomotive building company in the world. As the science of railway locomotive engineering progressed, steam locomotives increased in size and power, and many of the most famous ever made were constructed in Glasgow. Sadly, the North British Locomotive Company, largest in Europe, passed into history with its closure in 1962.

As the locomotive market expanded, construction demand from overseas grew; the railways of India and Africa, in particular, becoming the North British Locomotive Company's best customers. Glaswegians, especially in the Springburn and Queen's Park areas of the city, became used to the sight of massive out-of-gauge steam locomotives being hauled by road through the streets en route to the docks for shipment overseas. This was the only viable means of transportation from the various works to the docks, as the wheel gauge of the country or railway company which had ordered the locomotives often differed from the 4' 8½", or "Standard", gauge used on all British main railways.

Although thousands of locomotives built in Glasgow became the mainstay of some of the railway networks throughout the World, the USA being the major exception, large numbers were also built for the home market. The first locomotives to be produced by the various Glasgow builders were for local customers. As railway networks spread nation-wide, orders spread throughout the British Isles over the years. Scotland, like England, started off with small railways, such as the Monkland and Kirkintilloch Railway, opened for traffic in October 1826, or the even earlier Kilmarnock and Troon Railway, opened in 1811. In terms of revenue some of these were more successful than others, and eventually amalgamations took place, culminating in five major Scottish railway companies: the Caledonian Railway; the North British Railway; the Glasgow and South Western Railway; the Highland Railway; and the Great North of Scotland Railway.

All major railway companies, plus certain industrial companies had continuous requirements for steam motive power. So in what became known as the Railway Age, the locomotive manufacturers of Glasgow prospered, until the age of the motor car and the jet plane eventually replaced their products.

Queen's Park Works, circa 1950.

The First Steam Locomotives

Following the invention of the steam engine, efficiency in many industries improved beyond recognition. The early steam engines were very primitive compared to those that followed and were prone to breakdown. In extreme cases they were liable to explode. However, engineers learned from these experiences, and managed to overcome the problems encountered in the handling of high-pressure steam. These problems included its application to the driving of machines which powered secondary equipment and their solution eventually revolutionised prior methods. The first steam engines were used for driving machine tools, pumps, looms and in fact anything that required continuous rotational movement. Later they progressed to eccentric motion as adaptability improved. In the beginning, all such steam engines were stationary, as they had to be close to supplies of coal and water. When they began to be used to supply the power for the propulsion of ships, coal and water were carried aboard. The advent of the railways, however, presented problems: firstly of how to reduce the weight of the engine itself, and secondly to transport it in a self-sufficient way carrying its own fuel. The first locomotives ran on roads, but their use as a means of transportation of goods and people was hampered by the extremely poor quality of the available roads. Also such engines would require to generate considerable power and traction to move themselves, let alone tow any other vehicles. Early railways were laid to follow comparatively flat routes, whereas most roads of the time had gradients, even the most moderate of which created difficulties for the early steam locomotive.

The inventor of the first railway steam locomotive was Richard Trevithick, born in 1771, the son of a Cornish mining engineer. His first experiments with steam powered vehicles, around 1800, were with road carriages not designed to run on rails. His first attempt ended in disaster with his steam powered carriage being totally devoured by fire.

Scotland's First Railway

The first railway in Scotland was in fact a wooden-railed wagonway, which predated the steam locomotive by 82 years, being laid down in 1722. It ran from Tranent to Cockenzie about ten miles east of Edinburgh. Part of it was disputed in a battle against Bonnie Prince Charlie on the 21st of September 1745. The wooden rails were replaced by iron ones in 1815. Around 1880 it was converted into a colliery railway with steam power.

From such humble beginnings spread the railway network in Scotland. As with England, Scotland's earliest railways were industrial until the implications of using railways as a public service were realised. As there were no Scottish locomotive builders at this time, the earliest Scottish railway lines imported their locomotives from England, many of them built by Robert Stephenson & Co.

Garnkirk & Glasgow Railway No. 4 'Gartgill'. 12^{1}/$_{2}$" 0-6-0, with 3'9" driving wheels, built by Murdoch, Aitken & Co. in 1833. East Dumbartonshire Libraries. Courtesy of the Trustees of the late James F McEwan.

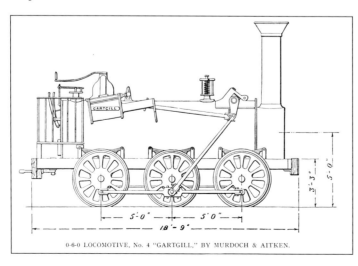

0-6-0 LOCOMOTIVE, No. 4 "GARTGILL," BY MURDOCH & AITKEN.

Murdoch, Aitken & Co

The date of origin of this firm is unclear, but for some time after its foundation it was a general engineering firm producing pumps, machine tools, and marine, high pressure and stationary steam engines. Its Works were at Hill Street Foundry in Glasgow, and it was the first firm to receive an order for steam railway locomotives in Scotland. As such Murdoch, Aitken & Co. laid the foundation of what was to become one of Glasgow's major industries. That historic first order was for the construction of two locomotives, of 0-4-0 wheel arrangement, for the Monkland and Kirkintilloch Railway. The first was completed in May 1831 and the second in September of the same year. This order was followed by one from the Garnkirk and Glasgow Railway, which had opened to the public on 27th September 1831, for an 0-6-0, a 2-2-0, and an 0-4-0, which were duly completed in 1833, 1834 and 1836 respectively. Further orders came from the Paisley and Renfrew Railway and the Slamannan Railway, with one order for an 0-4-0 for the London and Southampton Railway, probably the first locomotive built in Glasgow for outwith Scotland. This locomotive functioned until 1848 when it was wrecked beyond repair in a collision.

Murdoch, Aitken & Co. seem to have built reliable engines, but following the completion of an 0-4-0 for the Slamannan Railway in 1841, construction ceased. In view of what the Glasgow locomotive industry was to become, it can only be a matter of speculation as to what success they may have achieved had they persisted. The designs for their locomotives had been submitted by the engineers of the railway companies placing the orders, and were on the whole based on locomotives built by Robert Stephenson & Co. Some of the designs were improved versions of the by now famous "Rocket".

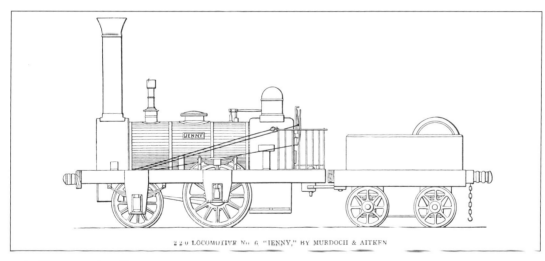

2-2-0 LOCOMOTIVE No. 6 "JENNY," BY MURDOCH & AITKEN

Planet-type 2-2-0. The first engines of this type were built by Robert Stephenson & Co. and introduced on the Liverpool and Manchester Railway in 1830-31. This example was built by Murdoch, Aitken & Co. for the Garnkirk & Glasgow Railway in 1836. East Dunbartonshire Libraries. Courtesy of the Trustees of the late James F McEwan.

Neilson & Co

Neilson & Co was one of the three locomotive building firms which eventually became part of the North British Locomotive Company, and was the first of the three to be founded in Glasgow. Walter Montgomerie Neilson, born 1819 in Glasgow, was a man with enough vision to see that a thriving railway industry would require a continuing supply of steam locomotives, and decided to enter the field of locomotive construction. The foundations were laid down for him, because he came from a family experienced in the manufacture of stationary and marine steam engines. His father, James Beaumont Neilson, revolutionised the manufacture of iron by devising the "Hot Blast" method used successfully from 1828; and his uncle, John Neilson, was responsible for building the "Fairy Queen", the first iron ship made to grace the Clyde, in 1831. Thus Walter had been exposed to some major innovations in engineering from his earliest childhood. In 1836 his cousin William Neilson, together with James Mitchell, founded the general engineering firm of Neilson & Mitchell in Hyde Park Street, in the Finnieston area of Glasgow.

This type of firm had become common in most industrialised areas of Britain by the early 1830s owing to a growing need to produce engines which could do the work of men more efficiently. The costs of establishing the firm were largely met by James Beaumont Neilson. This may account for the fact that in 1838 Walter entered the firm as a partner aged 17, having left the employ of the St. Rollox Foundry Co. before the end of his apprenticeship. As a partner in Neilson & Mitchell, he completed his apprenticeship prior to the departure of both William Neilson and James Mitchell. James Beaumont Neilson, in partnership with Stewart Kerr, began a new firm at the same premises and gained a solid reputation for supplying high quality engines to factories. Despite this the company was losing money and closure was considered. They made several attempts to sell the business, without success. James Beaumont Neilson, no doubt concerned about his investment, went to some lengths to persuade Walter, still only 24, to take over the company. In this he was aided by James Mitchell, who returned as a partner to look after the financial aspects of the company. The name of Neilson & Mitchell was retained until 1855 when it became Neilson & Co.

Looking to diversify, Walter Montgomerie Neilson decided to branch out into the construction of steam locomotives as early as 1844. Acutely conscious of the burgeoning railway industry spreading across Scotland, and equally aware that all the equipment including locomotives was being made in England, Neilson saw that there was a service he could supply to the Scottish railways on their own doorstep. However, as orders materialised slowly he proceeded cautiously, continuing to manufacture the original products of his firm for a number of years until he felt that the locomotive building aspect was strong enough to be the sole means of profitably supporting Neilson & Co.

Before making his decision to concentrate on steam locomotive building, Neilson built up a team of competent directors and supervisors around him. It was around this time that he made decisions which he strongly regretted during the later life of his company. In 1852 Neilson appointed James Reid, born in1823 at Kilmaurs, Ayrshire, as his works manager. Prior to his appointment Reid had gained considerable experience in the general engineering field, but had no experience with the building of steam locomotives. So eventually, Neilson determined to replace him with someone who had the required knowledge. To this end, six years later Neilson appointed Henry Dübs as his new works manager, an appointment which was to prove quite short term. Dübs may have had the necessary experience, but preceding his arrival at the Hyde Park Works, he had been dismissed by one of the locomotive building firms in England, Beyer, Peacock & Co. of Manchester, because he was judged to be too easy-going. Disregarding this, Neilson made Dübs a partner in his firm. One advantage that Dübs conferred was access to persons influential in placing orders for locomotives. This proved useful to Neilson, as he had found it extremely difficult to break into a market which was completely dominated by English companies. Indeed according to Neilson himself, had it not been for the orders placed with him by Scottish railways, he would have found it virtually impossible to survive.

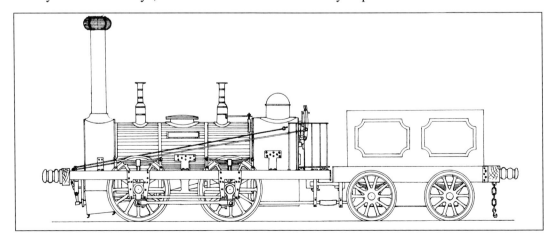

0-4-0 engine supplied to the Garnkirk & Glasgow Railway in 1843. The first locomotive built by Kerr, Mitchell & Neilson, predecessors of Neilson & Co.

As orders escalated space available at the Hyde Park Works became too small. Consequently, during his short tenure with Neilson & Co., Dübs was to mastermind one huge and complicated operation; the removal of the company premises to Springburn, in the north-east of Glasgow. There is some confusion as to whether the new works, retaining the Hyde Park Works name, was in fact laid out by Neilson or Dübs. Neilson claimed the credit, but the North British Locomotive Company's official history, published in 1953 to mark its fiftieth anniversary, credits Dübs. The move was completed in 1862. All the heavy equipment including planers, slotting machines, shaping machines, lathes, and three steam hammers had to be transported the several miles from the old premises to the new. This was achieved by the men who were employed in the works, using wagons and horses. As the route led up the hills of High Street, Castle Street, and Springburn Road, the men had to assist the horses by hauling on ropes, and the publicans on the route probably did some good business. Presumably the horses were given only water. Following the completion of the move to Springburn, and the recommencement of locomotive construction, the firm prospered. However, the relationship between Neilson and Dübs, which on a personal level does not appear to have been too good at the best of times, was now about to break down completely. Neilson had a poor opinion of Dübs as an engineer and the pair eventually parted company in 1863: Dübs, much to Neilson's chagrin, to set up his own independent works in Glasgow.

There now re-enters the scene James Reid, the same James Reid who had been manager of the old works in Finnieston, and had by now gained the necessary locomotive construction experience with the firm of Sharp, Stewart & Co. in Manchester. In 1863 he became the replacement for Henry Dübs, and was made a partner by Neilson for a period of ten years. This was to be Neilson's eventual undoing, for although the pair were successful as far as the prosperity of Neilson & Co. was concerned, there was a clause in Reid's contract which gave him the option of buying Neilson out, an option which it was understood that Reid would never exercise. By 1876 Neilson found himself completely cut off from the firm which he had done so much to establish as one of Britain's leading locomotive builders. He was, needless to say, extremely bitter and disillusioned by these events and claimed that Reid did not even pay him the amount of settlement agreed in the option. Walter Montgomerie Neilson was later to make another, not too successful, attempt to revive his fallen fortunes.

James Reid 1823-1894.

Henry Dübs 1816-1876.

Walter Montgomerie Neilson 1819-1889.

Under Reid's direction the firm, which retained the name of Neilson & Co. until 1898, when it was renamed Neilson, Reid & Co., continued to prosper, although it now had a great deal of competition from rival firms, both at home and abroad. James Reid died in 1894, during an arduous game of golf at St. Andrews. By the amalgamation in 1903, Neilson, Reid & Co. was the largest private locomotive building firm in Britain.

The Cowlairs Incline Winding Engine

The construction of the Edinburgh and Glasgow Railway line involved all the usual problems – with one major addition. From Cowlairs to Edinburgh was comparatively plain sailing, but the one and a half mile distance from Cowlairs to the heart of Glasgow at George Square, to be served by Queen St Station, was another matter entirely. The severe problem of the incline between these two points was solved by the creation of a tunnel, starting off as a cutting west of Cowlairs. The work took two and a half years. At its lower end it exited a few hundred yards from the station platforms. After the excavation and track laying, it was found that the gradient of the incline was so steep, varying from 1 in 41 to 1 in 50, that the locomotives of the day were not powerful enough to haul even the lightest of trains up to Cowlairs. The problem was solved by attaching ropes to the front of the locomotives and hauling them and their trains up the incline by means of a massive stationary steam engine.

To this end, a stone engine house with a 90 foot chimney was built at the top of Cowlairs Incline and was to become a landmark for travellers to and from Edinburgh for over seventy years. The steam engine, a gigantic twin-beam machine with two cylinders each 28" by 72" in size, was ordered from Neilson & Co. and installed in late 1841. It supplied power to an endless rope, approximately three miles long, to which the trains leaving Queen Street Station were attached at the entrance to the tunnel. Although the ropes were made of hemp and susceptible to breakages, trains were prevented from running backwards down the incline by

The engine house and winding engine of the Cowlairs Incline Winding Engine.

extremely powerful brakes. The railway opened for traffic on 18th February 1842, but by mid-1843 the ropes were causing such problems that it was decided that some other method of getting the trains up the incline must be attempted. Accordingly, the Edinburgh and Glasgow Railway constructed at its Cowlairs Works two locomotives named "Hercules" and "Sampson"; reckoned to be the most powerful in the world at the time. These engines, each weighing 26½ tons, were at first extremely successful, but soon created a new problem in that their weight was excessive for even the best quality iron rails of the day. Rail breakages became common. The return to rope haulage was inevitable, but this time the rope used was one of untwisted wire made by Robert Stirling Newall. The Neilson engine was fired up again for its second period of service on 4th March 1847. It ran more or less continually for another sixty-two years until the development of locomotives powerful enough to haul trains up the Incline by their own efforts. The engine's longevity is surely a tribute to the quality of workmanship produced by Neilson & Co. It may also have had something to do with the care lavished on it by the man who was in charge of it for no less than fifty-two years, Mr. George Jack.

The Locomotives Neilson & Co. Built for Britain

As Neilson recorded, he would have been hard pressed to establish a foothold in the locomotive building market had it not been for the early Scottish railways. The first examples of his designs to emerge from the Hyde Park Works in Finnieston were three 0-4-0s, built for the Garnkirk and Glasgow Railway in 1843 and named respectively "Alchemist", "Astrologer", and "Magician". This was quickly followed by orders almost exclusively from fledgling Scottish railways: the Monkland and Kirkintilloch Railway; the Wishaw and Coltness Railway; the Glasgow and Ayr Railway; the Edinburgh and Glasgow Railway; the Ardrossan Railway; the Caledonian Railway; the Troon Railway Co.; the Morayshire Railway; and the Glasgow and South Western Railway. All these orders were placed before 1855 and were interspersed with orders for industrial railways, again more or less entirely from Scotland. The first English order for Neilson & Co. was from the Furness Railway, who placed several orders, followed by contracts from the Eastern Counties Railway, in 1859. Until the mid-1860s there were repeat orders from many of the earlier Scottish customers, and new ones from the Edinburgh, Perth and Dundee Railway; the North British Railway; the Scottish Central Railway; the Inverness and Aberdeen Railway; and several Irish railways. From the resiting to Springburn until the amalgamation, orders from British railways, each for varying numbers of locomotives, rolled in as follows:

43 from the Caledonian Railway; 2 from the Cambrian Railway; 1 from the Colne Valley Railway; 2 from the Dingwall and Skye Railway; 1 from the Girvan and Portpatrick Railway; 1 from the Glasgow and Paisley Railway; 4 from the Great Central Railway; 14 from the Glasgow and South Western Railway; 10 from the Great Eastern Railway; 7 from the Great Northern Railway; 9 from the Great North of Scotland Railway; 1 from the Highland Railway; 3 from the Lancashire and Yorkshire Railway; 2 from the London, Brighton and South Coast Railway; 5 from the London, Chatham and Dover Railway; 8 from the London and South Western Railway; 6 from the Manchester, Sheffield and Lincoln Railway; 2 from the Maryport and Carlisle Railway; 1 from the Metropolitan Railway; 17 from the Midland Railway; 11 from the North British Railway; 3 from the North Eastern Railway; 1 from the North Staffordshire Railway; 1 from the Rhymney Railway; 2 from the Scottish North Eastern Railway; 2 from the Somerset and Dorset Railway; 8 from the South Eastern Railway; 2 from the South Eastern and Chatham Railway; and 1 from the Taff Vale Railway. There were also 19 orders for various Irish railways.

Many of these locomotives reflected the most advanced aspects of railway technology and hauled the crack express trains of the day. Some were workhorses, moving freight trains throughout their networks, while others were small simple shunting engines. Many of the

Edinburgh & Glasgow Railway No. 88. Former Caledonian & Dumbartonshire Junction Railway 10" 2-2-2 tank engine, with 5'0" driving wheels. Built by Neilson & Co. in 1850.

latter two types had long working lives, but because their roles were more menial they were not expected to impress the public who travelled by train on main routes – a public with an ever increasing demand for the decrease in travelling time between major cities.

Caledonian Railway No. 123

Perhaps the best known locomotive ever to emerge from the Hyde Park Works of Neilson & Co., Caledonian Railway No. 123, was a true one of a kind. Originally built by Neilson & Co. to their own specifications to represent the firm at the Edinburgh Exhibition of 1886, the locomotive, which was of 4-2-2 wheel arrangement, was sold to the Caledonian Railway. It had 18"x 26" cylinders, driving wheels 7' 0" in diameter, leading and rear wheels of 3' 6" diameter, weighed 41 tons 18 cwt in full working order, and had a boiler working pressure of 150 pounds per square inch. Its first claim to fame was the part it played in the "Railway Races" of 1888. In an increasingly competitive world, the railway companies responsible for transporting passengers from London to Edinburgh, and from there to Aberdeen, were determined to outdo each other in how quickly they could get their respective passengers to the required Scottish destinations. The east coast route trains departed from King's Cross Station and travelled to Edinburgh by way of Grantham, York, Newcastle, and Berwick, while the west coast trains left from Euston Station and went north via Crewe, Preston and Carlisle. There had always been a strong rivalry between the companies on each route, a rivalry which was not only concerned with revenue, but also with the matter of pride. The races materialised due to first one company cutting their travelling time from London, which led to their rivals cutting their journey time, resulting in the first competitor decreasing travel time again, and so on. This led to obvious practical difficulties in that the railway companies who covered each route had to co-operate to the second with each other. Their locomotives had to be the most powerful available, and the timetables had to be strictly adhered to. If a train arrived early at a designated passenger pick-up point, such as York, it could not leave until the time of departure advertised in the timetable. For the Scottish section of the race, responsibility lay with the North British Railway for the east coast trains and with the Caledonian Railway for the west coast route. First into Edinburgh, a bastion of North British Railway territory, was able to gain the advantage for the final part of the race to Aberdeen. The whole journey, including stops and changes of locomotives, eventually took less than eight hours, a travelling time not to be repeated until the advent of diesel and electric motive power.

On August 6th 1888, the honour of hauling the train from Carlisle to Edinburgh fell to No. 123. Booked on a scheduled timing of 112 minutes for the 100.6 mile run, 123 ran from Carlisle to the Caledonian Railway's Princes Street Station in Edinburgh in 104 minutes. The locomotive continued to haul the same train throughout the month of August 1888, with an average speed of journeys over the month of 56 miles per hour. The races continued until 1895, with final victory going to the east coast railways.

Caledonian Railway no. 123, following its historic performances in the races, continued to be a showpiece locomotive. From the beginning of the twentieth century until this Railway's demise with the "Grouping" in 1923, this locomotive was the Royal Pilot Engine which preceded any trains carrying royal personages over Caledonian Railway metals. Until 1935 when withdrawn from service, 123 was a good servant to the London, Midland and Scottish Railway. It was then restored to its original condition, repainted in its glorious Caledonian blue livery and used to haul special trains, sometimes on its own and sometimes in tandem with one or other of three preserved Glasgow built engines: Highland Railway "Jones Goods" 4-6-0 no. 103; North British Railway 4-4-0 no. 256 "Glen Douglas"; or Great North of Scotland Railway 4-4-0; "Gordon Highlander". Today all four are preserved in majestic splendour on display in Glasgow's Museum of Transport, reminders of an era when the steam locomotive reigned supreme.

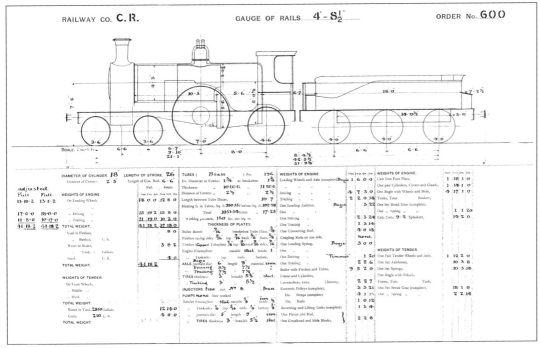

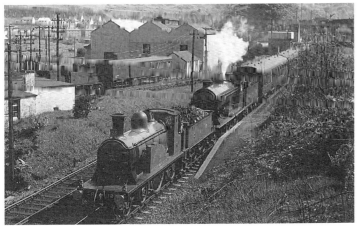

(Above) Weight diagram of Caledonian Railway No. 123.

*(Left) Preserved Caledonian Railway No. 123 and preserved North British Railway 'Glen' class 4-4-0 'Glen Douglas' passing Oban engine shed on the last official steam-hauled train from Glasgow to Oban in May 1962.
C L Kerr Collection, The Mitchell Library.*

14   Glasgow: Locomotive Builder to Britain

(Above) Great North of Scotland Railway No. 47. Cowan 16" 4-4-0, with 5'6½" coupled wheels. One of 6 built by Neilson & Co. in 1865-66.

Caledonian Railway No. 35. Conner 17" 2-4-0, with 7'2" driving wheels. One of 6 built by Neilson & Co. in 1872.

Great Central Railway No. 1052. Robinson 19" 0-8-0, with 4'7" wheels. One of 3 built by Neilson, Reid & Co. in 1902.

London & South Western Railway No. 636. Adams 18" 0-4-2, with 6'0" driving wheels. One of 40 built by Neilson & Co. in 1892.

Great Eastern Railway No. 539. Adams 19" 2-6-0, with 4'0" coupled wheels. One of 15 built by Neilson & Co. in 1878-79. The first engines with 2-6-0, 'Mogul', wheel arrangement to run in Great Britain.

North British Railway No. 496 'Helensburgh'. Drummond 17" 4-4-0T, with 6'0" coupled wheels. One of 3 supplied by Neilson & Co. in 1879.

Dübs & Co.

After leaving Neilson & Co., Henry Dübs began the process of creating his own locomotive building works, which would inevitably be in direct competition with that of his former partner. He had agreed with Neilson that establishment of such a works would be situated not less than three miles from Hyde Park Works. Accordingly, Dübs found a site in the Queen's Park area of Polmadie, on a corner of Aikenhead Road and Calder Street. The back of this site overlooked the main railway line from Glasgow Central Station to Carlisle and the south and thus gave Dübs easy access to a rail link by which locomotives built for the home railways could be delivered. Henry Dübs was born in Darmstadt, Germany in 1816. As a trained engineer, he was employed by the English locomotive building firm of Beyer, Peacock & Co., of Manchester. Charles F. Beyer, a founder, was born in Saxony, and employed a number of his fellow countrymen, including Dübs. Clearly much more capable and ambitious than Walter Neilson believed, Dübs designed and built his own factory from scratch, personally cutting the first sod in April 1864. He used the clay from the foundations to make the bricks for the buildings, and on each brick was stamped the diamond-shaped trademark with which all his locomotives were later endowed. A version of this was to become the recognised trademark of the North British Locomotive Company. He equipped his new premises with brand new, state-of-the-art machinery. Within a year the new Glasgow Locomotive Works were ready for production and the orders quickly began to roll in. One of the reasons for his former employment with Neilson & Co. was that Neilson wanted Dübs for his contacts, which he used to help obtain orders. With the start of his own firm, Dübs now used his many contacts for his own ends, much to Neilson's dismay. Not only did Neilson lose the benefits of Dübs' personal knowledge and friendship in the locomotive market, he lost a number of his key staff as well. The most notable of these was Sampson George Goodall-Copestake, his chief draughtsman, whom Dübs persuaded, probably for higher wages, to join him in his new venture. Goodall-Copestake later became a partner.

　　One of the innovations which Dübs introduced was the employment of women as drawing tracers, since he reckoned that women would be better at carrying out this task than men. The engineering profession was profoundly shocked at this invasion by women into a male stronghold, and protested strongly. However, Dübs ensured that propriety was observed, and women employees were segregated from the male workers. The practice continued throughout the existence of Dübs & Co., and following its merger into the North British Locomotive Company, until the closure of that firm. There are still some former tracers around today, and they relate that even in the 1960s it was frowned upon for the women to have any dealings with the men during working hours. Apart from the fact that Dübs was correct, and that women were better than men at the job, the practice was continued after Dübs' death, in 1876. Managerial control of the firm then passed into the hands of William Lorimer, who had joined Dübs as principal assistant in 1864 becoming a partner in 1875. Working with tracers throughout his career he presumably shared Dübs' esteem for them, as when he became the first Chairman of the North British Locomotive Company he continued to employ women in this capacity.

During its existence until amalgamation, the firm built many locomotives for railway companies at home and abroad, including some of the first to run on new railways springing up across the world. The one thing that may have given Neilson some satisfaction, considering the bad relationship and injustices he considered he had suffered because of Dübs, was that while Dübs & Co. went on to become the second largest locomotive builder in Britain, Neilson & Co. remained top of the heap.

Group of tracers circa 1900.

Built by Dübs & Co. for Britain

Dübs & Co.'s best customers were overseas railways, but the firm received its share of orders from British railways, some of which may have gone to Neilson & Co. had there not been a parting of the ways. Many of the railway companies which placed orders with Neilson in the early days had been swallowed up by take-overs. Therefore, when Dübs & Co. began production, there were fewer customers but each of them was larger. Also quality standards had been set before Dübs founded his own firm, and he was able to produce high quality locomotives right from the start. Locomotive orders for British railways, again for varying numbers of locomotives, were as follows.

> 31 from the Caledonian Railway; 1 from the Glasgow, Barrhead and Kilmarnock Railway; 1 from the Glasgow, Hamilton and Bothwell Railway; 6 from the Glasgow and South Western Railway; 3 from the Great Eastern Railway; 5 from the Great Northern Railway; 9 from the Highland Railway; 1 from the Jersey Railway; 2 from the Lancashire and Yorkshire Railway; 1 from the London, Brighton and South Coast Railway; 2 from the London, Chatham and Dover Railway; 3 from the London, Tilbury and Southend Railway;

5 from the London and South Western Railway; 1 from the Manx Northern Railway; 19 from the Midland Railway; 5 from the Midland and South Western Junction Railway; 1 from the North Staffordshire Railway; 9 from the North British Railway; 3 from the North Eastern Railway; 1 from the South Eastern Railway; 1 from the South Eastern and Chatham Railway; and 1 from the Swindon and Marlborough Railway. 27 orders were also received from Irish railways.

Comparison with Neilson & Co. shows that the former received 172 orders from British railways with 19 from Ireland, while Dübs & Co. received 112 and 27 respectively. From the local railway companies in and around Springburn, Neilson & Co. received 43 orders from the Caledonian as against 31 by Dübs. Many of the orders received by Dübs & Co. were from customers who had been with Neilson & Co. previously. Some customers continued to place orders with both firms, but the number of potential orders which Neilson lost to Dübs can only be imagined.

Highland Railway No. 67 'The Duke'. Jones 18" 4-4-0, with 6'3¹/₂" coupled wheels. One of 10 supplied by Dübs & Co. in 1874. The first new-build 'Crewe' type 4-4-0s to run to Great Britain.

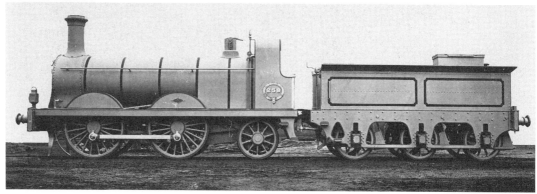

Glasgow & South Western Railway No. 259. 18" 0-4-2, with 5'7¹/₂" coupled wheels. One of 10 supplied by Dübs & Co. 1876.

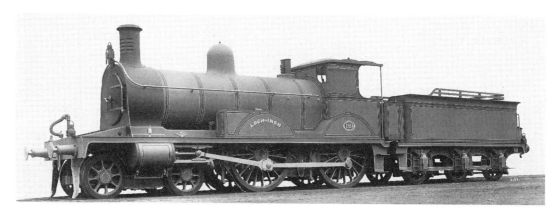

Highland Railway No. 119 'Loch Insh'. Jones 19" 4-4-0 'Loch' class, with 6'3¹/₂" coupled wheels. One of 15 built by Dübs & Co. in 1896.

(Above) Manx Northern Railway No. 4 'Caledonia'. 13¹/₂" 0-6-0T, with 3'3" wheels.
Built by Dübs & Co. in 1885.

(Left) Caledonian Railway No. 124. Drummond 19" 4-4-0, with 6'6" driving wheels. Special exhibition locomotive built for the Edinburgh Exhibition of 1886 by Dübs & Co. Fitted with Bryce-Douglas valve gear.

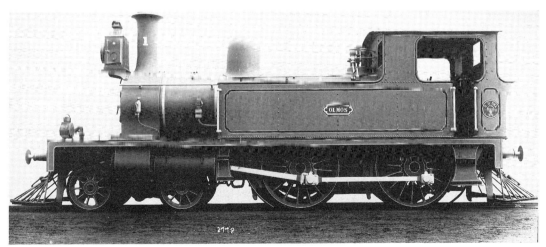

Highland Railway No. 101 16" 4-4-0T, with 5'3" driving wheels. One of 2 built by Dubs & Co. in 1890-91 for the Uruguay Great Eastern Railway, but not supplied. Both engines were sold to the Highland Railway in 1893.

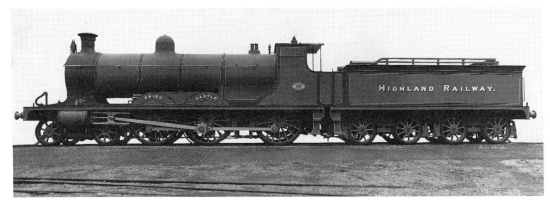

Highland Railway No. 146 'Skibo Castle'. Peter Drummond 19$\frac{1}{2}$" 4-6-0 'Castle' class, with 5'9" coupled wheels. One of 4 supplied by Dübs & Co. in 1902.

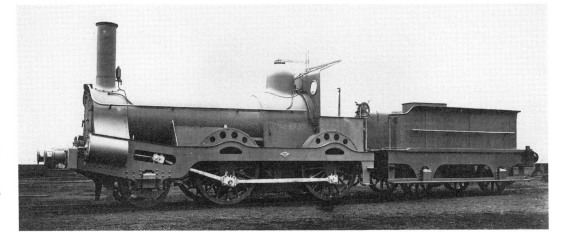

Caledonian Railway 17" 2-4-0, with 5'2" coupled wheels. One of 6 supplied by Dübs & Co. in 1865.

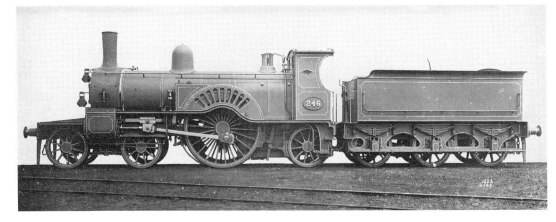

Great Eastern Railway No. 246. Bromley 18" 4-2-2, with 7'6" driving wheels. One of 10 built by Dübs & Co. in 1879.

Highland Railway No. 1, later named 'Ben Nevis'. Peter Drummond 18$\frac{1}{4}$" 4-4-0 'Small Ben' class, with 6'0" coupled wheels. One of 8 supplied by Dübs & Co. in 1897.

"Bens", "Castles" and "Lochs"

Probably the most famous railway locomotives built by Dübs & Co. for the home market were the "Ben" class 4-4-0s and the "Castle" class 4-6-0s built for the Highland Railway. The "Bens" or more correctly, "Small Bens", were the first locomotives designed by Peter Drummond following his appointment as locomotive superintendent of the Highland Railway in 1896. The first eight examples of the class, each named after a Highland mountain, were supplied by Dübs & Co. from 1898 to 1899. They were of 4-4-0 wheel arrangement and carried Highland Railway running numbers 1-8 owing to a complete renumeration process by the Highland Railway. They were less powerful versions of the earlier "Loch" class 4-4-0s, designed by David Jones, Drummond's predecessor, and the first fifteen were built by Dübs & Co. in 1896. While they were used on the Highland main line from Inverness to the south, the smaller "Bens" also did sterling work on the Inverness to Wick line. This less powerful type was also used fairly constantly on the line running east from Inverness to Aberdeen. Several of them lasted through the Grouping of 1923, and some even survived for a few years after British Railways came into existence in 1948. The last to be withdrawn from active service was Highland Railway no. 2 (Dübs works number 3686) "Ben Alder", built in July 1898 and withdrawn as British Railways no. 54398 in February 1953. "Ben Alder" lasted long after withdrawal and languished for many years in a somewhat dilapidated state in Dawsholm Shed in Glasgow before finally being scrapped some time in the late 1960s. It had originally been scheduled for permanent preservation, but the funding never materialised.

The Highland Railway "Castle" class, named after Highland castles, were 4-6-0 express passenger locomotives developed from the earlier "Jones Goods" locomotives. The first six were supplied by Dübs & Co. in 1900, and a further four in 1902. They worked the cream of the Highland Railway expresses on the Inverness to Perth line. Here their superior power was heavily exploited on the severe climb, south of Inverness, up the very steep gradient to Slochd Summit and on the long climbs in both directions through the Grampians. As usual with Dübs locomotives, they performed well in all that was required of them. Several continued in service with the London, Midland and Scottish Railway until the mid-1940s.

"Oban Bogies"

Another Scottish railway which had its fair share of steep gradients, and was well served by Dübs locomotives, was the Callander and Oban. This line took approximately fourteen years to build before finally opening in 1880. At Oban, from the station at the North Pier, trains moved off towards the east from a standing start straight into a severe gradient which lasted for about three miles until the trains reached Glencruitten Summit. It was virtually impossible to reach any reasonable speed before the bottom of the incline. On wet days the rails could become especially greasy and slippery, and despite locomotives having sanding gear to help adhesion on the track, trains ground their way very slowly up the cutting, requiring great skill on the part of the drivers. Sometimes they failed and had to be shoved from the rear with the help of another locomotive.

The Caledonian railway company supplied the motive power and stock of the Callander and Oban Railway. Because of severe curvature on the line, locomotives could not be above a certain length and weight, and in the early days traffic on the line was hauled by tank rather than tender locomotives. The early tank locomotives were not really up to the job, and an order was placed with Dübs & Co. for ten 4-4-0 tender locomotives which were duly delivered to the Caledonian Railway in 1882. They became known as the "Oban Bogies", since they were the first engines on the Oban route which had leading bogies rather than the fixed wheels of the earlier tank engines. In addition to the curve limits, the overall length of the locomotive and tender was restricted by the dimensions of Oban's smallish turntable. Because the Callander and Oban Railway was of single track throughout its length, except for short passing places of double track usually at stations, each locomotive which hauled a train out had to be turned before it could haul a train back. The "Oban Bogies" were of the expected Dübs high quality and were well liked by their drivers as they were easy to steam. They successfully coped with the difficulties of the line until around the 1900s when trains became heavier as passenger and freight traffic increased. More powerful engines eventually replaced them, but the name "Oban Bogie" was retained, even though the later generations were of 4-6-0 wheel arrangement, some of them built by the North British Locomotive Company.

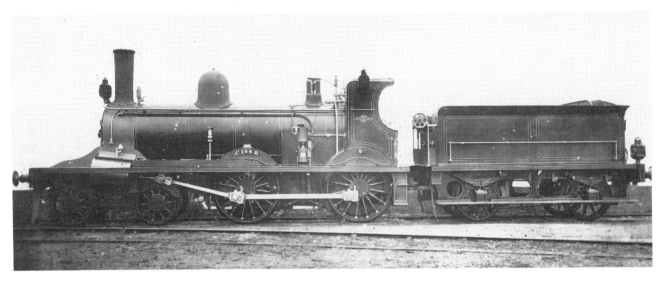

Caledonian Railway No. 188. Brittain 18" 'Oban Bogie', 4-4-0, with 5'2" coupled wheels. One of 10 built by Dübs & Co. in 1882.

The Clyde Locomotive Co.

Following his exodus from Neilson & Co. in 1876, Walter Montgomerie Neilson spent the next few years travelling abroad, perhaps in an effort to forget the wrongs he considered James Reid had done him. In spite of misfortunes operating his business Neilson was highly regarded as a first class engineer, and prior to his departure his assistance had been requested by Ferdinand de Lesseps to solve problems encountered in building the Suez Canal. Neilson's advice helped the canal to its successful completion, but he was not finished with the locomotive building trade yet. In 1884 he purchased land directly across the North British Railway's main line from his former works, and re-entered the business with a new firm, the Clyde Locomotive Company. Neilson had been absent from the scene for several years and now faced competition from Neilson & Co., Dübs & Co., and from elsewhere in Britain. New orders were difficult to obtain. During the firm's short existence, Neilson received only eight orders and built just fourteen locomotives between 1886, when the first was completed, and the end of 1887.

The Clyde Locomotive's first order was for a batch of eight locomotives for the Highland Railway. These eight were named "Clyde Bogies" by the railway, in honour of the firm which built them. The first of them, Highland Railway no. 76 "Bruce", was exhibited at the 1886 Edinburgh Exhibition where Neilson & Co. were represented by Caledonian Railway no. 123. The "Clyde Bogies" were fairly typical of the Highland Railway 4-4-0s of their day and gave good service. All except one were withdrawn from service with the introduction of the Grouping in 1923, the last withdrawn in April 1930. In addition to the Highland Railway locomotives, two 0-6-0 locomotives were built for the Ayr and Wigtownshire Railway, plus three small industrial tank locomotives, one for a Welsh ironworks.

It must have been extremely galling for Neilson, looking out from his sparsely productive works, to see the steady stream of new locomotives emerging from his former company across the main line, particularly as he had put so much effort into the creation and growth of that company. But, despite the comparative failure of the Clyde Locomotive Company, Walter Montgomerie Neilson was not finished yet.

Sharp, Stewart & Co.

This company of locomotive builders was the oldest of the three which were to become the North British Locomotive Company, and was well established long before it ever had any connections with Glasgow. Like many other pioneering locomotive builders, Sharp, Stewart & Co. had originally entered the field of mechanical engineering with the production of machine tools and large quantities of machinery for the local cotton mills. This had been in 1811 when the company name had been Sharp, Greenleaves & Co. and its works in New York Street, Manchester. With the spread of the early railways in England, the firm entered the field of locomotive building, and the first locomotive produced was a 2-2-0, aptly named "Experiment", which was supplied to the Liverpool and Manchester Railway in 1833. Earlier, in 1822, the company, which went through several changes of name before it finally became Sharp, Stewart & Co. in 1852, was known as Sharp, Roberts & Co., owing to an inventor and engineer by the name of Richard Roberts joining the board as a partner. He was responsible for the introduction and profusion of the injector into the British locomotive building industry. An injector is a device which feeds water into the boiler of a steam locomotive when the water content starts to run low. It had previously been used in France, but Roberts took out the British patent.

The next batch of locomotives built by Sharp, Roberts & Co. consisted of three 2-2-0s, known as the "Hibernia" class, which were supplied, in 1834, to the Dublin and Kingstown Railway, the first in Ireland. The firm continued to prosper, both in the field of locomotive building, and in its earlier production of machine tools, for unlike Walter Montgomerie Neilson, they did not concentrate exclusively on the construction of locomotives. However, the firm became very successful in this field, largely due to the building in 1837 of a 2-2-2 locomotive design, which was to become a standard type. Over the next twenty years around 600 standard types were built for many British railways as well as those of a number of European countries. They quickly became known as the "Sharp Singles" and were as famous in their day as any of the bigger and more powerful locomotives which were to follow.

Highland Railway No. 76 'Bruce'. Jones 18" 4-4-0 with 6'3½" coupled wheels. One of 8 'Clyde Bogies' supplied by the Clyde Locomotive Company in 1886. Photographed outside the Highland Railway's Lochgorm Works.

By the 1870s Sharp, Stewart & Co. were one of the leading manufacturers in England, if not Britain, and were perhaps on a par with Neilson & Co. and Dübs & Co. This may have resulted, to some extent, from the fact that the company had been in the business from the outset. Many of their customers being the early English railways, satisfied customers kept coming back to them with further contracts. Their market developed with the growth of the railways, whereas both Walter Neilson and Henry Dübs had to try to break into an already established market. This is especially true of Neilson who had great difficulty in getting English railway companies to believe in the integrity of his company in its early days. In 1887, however, Sharp, Stewart & Co. found themselves with a problem. The lease on their Manchester factory was about to run out and could not be renewed. Alternative premises were urgently required. The directors approached Walter Montgomerie Neilson at his ailing Clyde Locomotive Company, and an "agreement" was reached, which proved satisfactory to both parties. Not only would Sharp, Stewart & Co. gain new premises in an almost new and fully laid out works, but the rates of pay for Scottish labour were cheaper than those of their English counterparts. It would also be easier for them to ship locomotives built for export from the Clyde than it had been from Manchester, particularly as the locomotives of the time were increasing in size and weight. Neilson would have his outstanding orders completed for him, with the financial clout of the prosperous Sharp, Stewart & Co. bringing a major injection of much needed capital into his firm. It may be that Neilson had learned from his previous experiences, for, while he was not in overall control of the firm taking over his works, he insisted that a directorship offered to him was for life, with suitable remuneration. In this capacity he does not appear to have taken a very active part in Sharp, Stewart & Co.'s business in Glasgow. He resumed his travels and died in Florence on 8th July 1889, at the age of 69. Henry Dübs was long gone before the arrival of Sharp, Stewart & Co. in Glasgow in 1888, but James Reid was very much alive. His thoughts about the arrival of another fully fledged major locomotive building firm a few hundred yards from his own backyard are not known. Sharp, Stewart & Co. were in Glasgow to stay with their new works being named the Atlas Works, like their old premises in Manchester.

The Atlas Works was not the first railway works to occupy the former Clyde Locomotive Company site in Springburn. Part of the area had previously belonged to the early steam locomotive manufacturer, James M. Rowan & Co. who is said to have started building locomotives as far back as 1834. The Company's history is somewhat unclear, but from 1839 to 1851 it produced around a dozen locomotives for several local railways, starting with two 2-2-2s for the Slamannan Railway, followed by 0-4-0s for the Wishaw and Coltness Railway, the Pollok and Govan Railway, and the Monkland and Kirkintilloch Railway. The firm seems to have drifted out of locomotive building after that, but it is possible that their premises were bought by Walter Neilson before he set up the Clyde Locomotive Company.

With the move to Glasgow, Sharp, Stewart & Co's business expanded. Their new works had a capacity to build 150 locomotives at once, but they never quite fulfilled this potential. They did however, become the third largest steam locomotive builders in Britain, creating difficulties in later years, when they had to compete strongly with Neilson & Co. and Dübs & Co. for orders.

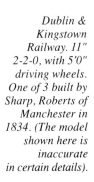

Dublin & Kingstown Railway. 11" 2-2-0, with 5'0" driving wheels. One of 3 built by Sharp, Roberts of Manchester in 1834. (The model shown here is inaccurate in certain details).

Grand Junction Railway 'Atlas'. 12¹/₂" 2-2-2, with 5'0" driving wheels. One of 10 built by Sharp, Roberts of Manchester in 1837. The first of the famous 'Sharp Single' type.

London & North Western Railway No. 249. McConnell 'Bloomer' type 16" 2-2-2, with 7'0" driving wheels. One of 10 built by Sharp Brothers of Manchester in 1851. Inside frames and bearings only.

British Locomotives Built in Glasgow by Sharp, Stewart & Co.

Many of the railway companies to whom Sharp, Stewart & Co. supplied locomotives after their move to Glasgow had been customers during their tenure in Manchester. New customers in Britain from 1888 were the Neath and Brecon Railway; the Midland and Great Northern Joint Railway; the Midland and South Western Junction Railway; the Metropolitan Railway; the Port Talbot Railway and Docks Company; and the Great Central Railway, all in England or Wales. Perhaps surprisingly, considering the longevity of the builders and the railway companies concerned, they also received their first orders from four of the major Scottish railways, two from the North British Railway, and one each from the Caledonian Railway, the Glasgow and South Western Railway, and the Highland Railway. In all their independent existence, Sharp, Stewart & Co. received not a single order from the fifth major Scottish railway, the Great North of Scotland Railway. The Highland Railway order in particular must have caused some concern to the two other major firms. Apart from the single order for the "Clyde Bogies" the two, especially Dübs & Co., seemed to have a virtual monopoly of supplying locomotives to the Highland, other than those which the company built themselves at their Lochgorm Works. The single order filled by Sharp, Stewart was a very important one in the historical development of the steam locomotive in Britain.

Southwold Railway No. 1 'Southwold'. 8" 2-4-2T, with 2'6" coupled wheels.
Built by Sharp, Stewart & Co. in 1893. 3'0" gauge.

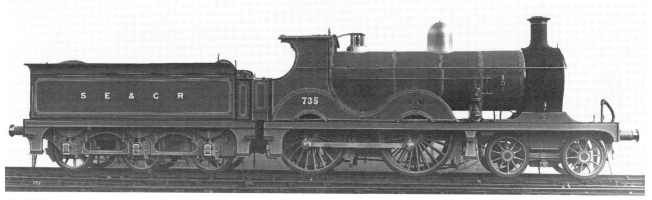

South Eastern & Chatham Railway No.735.Wainwright class 'D' 19" 4-4-0, with 6'8" coupled wheels. This locomotive,
completed by Sharp, Stewart & Co. in 1901, was exhibited at the Glasgow Exhibition of that year.

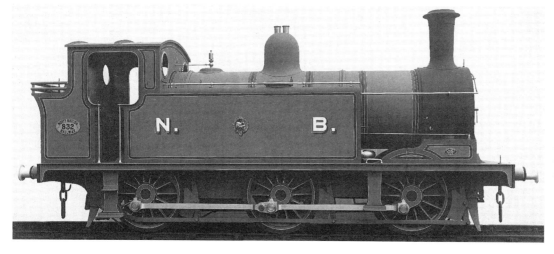

North British
Railway No. 832.
Holmes 17"
0-6-0T, with 4'6"
wheels. One of 20
built by Sharp,
Stewart & Co. in
1900-1.

London, Tilbury & Southend Railway No. 38 'Westcliff'. Thomas Whitelegg 18" 4-4-2T, with 6'6" coupled wheels. One of 6 supplied by Sharp, Stewart & Co. in 1897.

The "Jones Goods" 4-6-0s

The "Jones Goods" were the first steam locomotives of 4-6-0 wheel arrangement to be built for any railway company in Britain. This new arrangement meant that instead of the previous two or four driving wheels on a locomotive, there were now six, which allowed for heavier boilers of longer length, spread over a greater area above the driving wheels. The extra pair of wheels also gave better adhesion to the track, which meant that the additional power generated by the larger boiler could be used more efficiently to drive the engine, an important consideration on the steep lines of the Highland Railway. Fifteen of the engines were supplied by Sharp, Stewart & Co. in 1894 under their order number E1039, works numbers 4022-4036. They were named after their designer David Jones, who served the Highland Railway at Lochgorm Works for no less than forty-one years, until his forced retiral on 31st October 1896, due to an accident while testing a new locomotive. Born on 25th October 1834 in Manchester, Jones, some time after his recovery, moved to London, where he died in 1906 aged 72. He had designed a variety of locomotives for the Highland Railway, but his new goods locomotives were a radical departure from current locomotive practice anywhere in Britain at the time of their introduction. They were the most powerful locomotives yet to run on a British railway, with their 20" x 26" outside cylinders, their 5' 3" coupled driving wheels and a working boiler pressure of 175 pounds per square inch. In full working order each weighed 56 tons, of which 42 tons went into the provision of adhesion. Originally designed as freight engines, with heavy coal trains from the south especially in mind, their performance led to them also being used on passenger trains. They managed the steep inclines of the Highland main line from Perth, including the daunting Drumuachdar and Slochd gradients, with comparative ease. Nos. 103-117 on the Highland Railway, they became nos. 17916-19730 in the London, Midland and Scottish Railway. All of them were withdrawn from service by 1940, but No. 103 (17916) was later restored to its original condition and still exists today, surrounded by controversy in railway circles as to whether its restored livery is authentic.

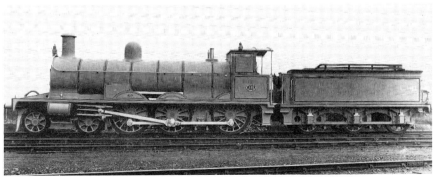

Highland Railway No. 111. 'Jones Goods' class 20" 4 6 0, with 5'3½" driving wheels. One of 15 supplied by Sharp, Stewart & Co. in 1894. The locomotives of this class were the first of 4-6-0 wheel arrangement built for service in Great Britain.

"Dunrobin"

Another engine, an 0-4-4 side tank locomotive, designed by David Jones for the privately owned railway of the Duke of Sutherland, was built by Sharp, Stewart & Co. in 1895. Named "Dunrobin" after the Duke's Highland residence, it was fitted with a leather seat to accommodate him and any of his guests who wanted to travel on the footplate of the engine. He also had a private coach which the locomotive hauled on occasion, both on his own railway and also on Highland metals. This was discontinued after nationalisation and the locomotive was sold to a Captain Howey in 1949 by the Duke's descendants. In 1965 it was shipped to Canada where it became the property of the British Columbian government, who put it on public display where, as far as is known, it remains.

The Duke of Sutherland's personal locomotive 'Dunrobin'. 13" 0-4-4T, with 4'6" coupled wheels. The Duke was allowed to run this locomotive over Highland Railway track between Dunrobin and Inverness. Built by Sharp, Stewart & Co. in 1895.

Glasgow and South Western Railway 381 class 4-6-0s

By the end of the nineteenth century, the Glasgow and South Western Railway's domain extended from: Glasgow St. Enoch Station in the north, west to Greenock, and south-west to Kilmarnock including the lucrative routes to the holiday resorts of Saltcoats, Troon, and Ayr on the Ayrshire coast. It also included the ferry port of Ardrossan, plus the main line from Kilmarnock to Dumfries and from thence to Carlisle, in other words most of south-west Scotland. The increasing weight of the trains, due to the greater number of passengers, was causing concern to the directors of the railway as more and more main line trains required either to be double-headed, or had to have the assistance of a pilot engine for climbing steep grades. Larger, more powerful locomotives were urgently needed. Accordingly the locomotive superintendent, James Manson, was ordered to draw up designs for improved locomotives. He submitted two designs, one for a 4-4-0 type, similar to but more powerful than the 4-4-0s which were the mainstay of the Glasgow and South Western's main line motive power until then, and one for a 4-6-0. Perhaps the Chairman, Partick Baird, had heard of the success of the "Jones Goods" on the Highland. In any case he immediately decided these were the engines to be built for the Glasgow and South Western Railway. Ten were ordered from Sharp, Stewart and Co. in 1902, under their order number E1202. While this was their Sharp, Stewart & Co. order number, their works numbers were allocated into the sequence to be followed by the soon to exist North British Locomotive Company (15734-15743). The engines were duly delivered in early summer 1903, becoming Glasgow and South Western Railway numbers 381-390. They were thirty per cent more powerful than the most powerful 4-4-0 on the line and had all the other advantages inherent in a 4-6-0. Among other features, these were the first locomotives in Scotland to be fitted with the successful Belpaire firebox. Because of their innovative design, teething troubles were at first encountered, but these were all ironed out by 1904, and the locomotives performed well on the express trains of the railway. By the end of World War I, and its heavy demands upon locomotives all over the nation to mobilise men and materials continually, the 381 class was in a bad state of disrepair and required rebuilding. Renovation completed, these engines continued to give good service up to London, Midland and Scottish Railway days.

Glasgow & South Western Railway No. 384. Manson 20" 4-6-0, with 6'6" coupled wheels. One of 10 ordered from Sharp, Stewart & Co. in 1902 but delivered by the North British Locomotive Co. in 1903.

The North British Locomotive Co.

By 1899 Neilson, Reid & Co., Dübs & Co., and Sharp, Stewart and Co. employed 3,275, 2,017 and 1,561 men respectively. Maintaining these employment levels required continuous orders to be coming in. The fact that the three companies were in competition with each other meant that they could not always individually obtain the best prices for their products. In spite of their business rivalry the directors of each of the three firms had a good relationship; facilitating the agreement that a merger was in their best interests. This process began in 1902 and on 1st April 1903 the North British Locomotive Company, later known in the trade as the "Combine", was officially born. The combined attributes of the new operation imbued Glasgow with the capability to build around 600 locomotives per year, all, as it were, under the same roof. From being the three largest locomotive building firms in Britain, the amalgamation created the third largest company in the world. Only Baldwin and the American Locomotive Company were bigger and much of their product was for the United States market, where British and European builders had never gained a foothold in any case. Much concern was shown by the other locomotive builders in Britain about the launch of the new giant. English firms such as Beyer, Peacock and Co. of Manchester, Kitson & Co. of Leeds, and Robert Stephenson & Co., which until 1903 had not been far behind the three Glasgow firms in size, suddenly found themselves having to compete with a leviathan which could produce three times more locomotives than they, and produce them cheaper and quicker. The North British Locomotive Company (NBL) now had a workforce of around 8,000 men and a combined site of sixty acres for completing orders. It could also split orders for large numbers of locomotives between three works. Although the NBL did not often build to capacity, for the first seven years of their operation an average of 500 locomotives per year emerged from the three sites.

The Chairman of the new company was William Lorimer, who had joined Dübs & Co. in 1864. Hugh Reid became Deputy Chairman and Chief Managing Director; Andrew Thomson Reid the Managing Director of the Hyde Park Works; William Lorimer, Junior, the Managing Director of the Queen's Park Works; John Hutchinson Sharp the Managing Director of the Atlas Works; and John Frederick Robinson the Managing Director of the firm's London office. There were four other directors, John Reid; Walter Montgomerie Neilson Reid; Alexander Wilson; and Charles Ralph Dübs. It is interesting to note, considering the way in which Walter Montgomerie Neilson and James Reid parted company, that the latter must have thought well of the former at one time to have named one of his sons Walter Montgomerie Neilson Reid.

It was not desirable to manage the operations of the three works as individual entities. A new building to focus the administration of the company was built in Flemington Street, facing the Hyde Park Works, and formally opened in 1909. During both World Wars, much of this building was used as a hospital for wounded troops, an additional contribution to the war efforts by a firm which produced munitions as well as locomotives. NBL even made artificial limbs for wounded soldiers. The Administration Building is one of the few reminders of the company remaining intact today. Now Glasgow North College it continues as a reminder of what life in Springburn was really about; the building of locomotives. Above its entrance doors there is still an effigy in stone, of the front of a locomotive. Many other indications of its origins remain such as the Memorial Window on its main staircase, which has been completely renovated within the last few years. The current principal of the college, Mr. Ian Miller, has a keen enthusiasm for the heritage of the building and what it once represented. Over the last few years the college has hosted three reunions of NBL employees, most recently in April 1997. While the numbers of ex-employees has dwindled now, since NBL closed its doors in 1962, these events have always been well attended. In some cases guests have travelled half-way across the world to be there, showing the strong affection that still exists for the company. The reunions were the brainchild of Mr. William Dewar, once in overall charge of locomotive transportation from the various works to the docks. He has an encyclopaedic knowledge of NBL and gives illustrated lectures on the firm and its history. The enthusiasm for the company which he and his ex-colleagues exude has to be experienced to be believed. It is to be hoped that the reunions continue for many years to come, as they represent the living history of a way of life which will never return.

From its auspicious formation in 1903 NBL prospered, with profits usually well in excess of £100,000 per annum, until World War I. 1920 and 1921 were NBL's best years as regards income, since many of their customers had to restock after the first World War. Then

The front entrance to 110, Flemington Street, showing the effigy of a locomotive carved in stone above the door.

came the Great Depression, which affected all the manufacturing industries. For several years in the late 1920s and the early 1930s profits could be counted in the low hundreds of pounds. Worse followed for 1934 -1938 showed the company running at a massive loss each year, peaking at almost £114,000 in 1936. Only the arrival of World War II rejuvenated NBL's fortunes, although never again would the halcyon days of the early 1920s return. Over and above the Depression in the late 1920s, the larger American builders had made serious inroads into the overseas market, and even had the audacity to attempt to gain orders in Britain, the birthplace of the steam locomotive. The size of NBL, a massive benefit when formed in 1903, now became a burden. The Atlas Works were closed and most of the staff made redundant. An attempt was made to sell the Atlas Works in 1927, but there were no buyers. In the other two works orders were being tendered for at a loss, in order to bring in some much needed capital, but here too the number of workers was being reduced, at a time when some of the most famous locomotives ever to run in Britain were being produced. After World War II, with nationalisation of the railways in 1948, orders were placed with NBL for new types of locomotives. Several orders required the building of more than a hundred of each type, with repeat orders to follow. Thus the North British Locomotive Company managed to survive, and survive quite well, albeit with their works now down to two from the original three of 1903. But in the early 1950s a new era was dawning, and although it would take a few years to reach fruition, it would ring the death-knell of NBL.

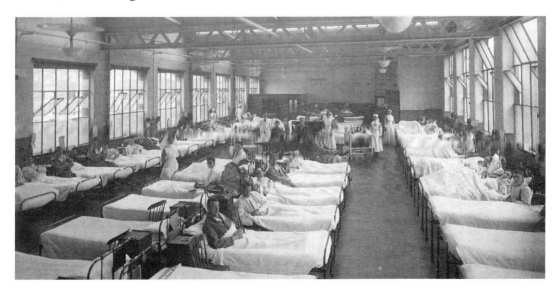

Part of the Administration Building was converted to a Military Hospital during the 1914-1918 War. This view shows the 'Springburn Ward'.

The rise of the petrol and diesel engine had gradually eroded the areas where the steam engine, and particularly the steam locomotive, had been king. Also, belief by the older directors of NBL that steam would remain the major source of power on the world's railways, especially in Asia, India, South America, and South Africa, made the board reluctant to diversify into new products. Government embargoes meant large orders numbering thousands of steam locomotives from both Russia and China never materialised. By the time it was agreed to examine the requirements necessary for a transition to the production of diesel and electric locomotives, the market had already been captured by some of NBL's previous rivals, and by new firms which sprang up in this field. Although NBL began, belatedly, to convert to the production of diesel locomotives in conjunction with the production of steam, railway companies from overseas, and even British Railways, were not interested in continuing with steam locomotives. The day came when steam production stopped at NBL, and problems encountered with their diesels meant that only a few short years elapsed before the company went into liquidation on 4th April 1962. The goodwill of the NBL passed to the comparatively small firm of Andrew Barclay, Sons & Co. of Kilmarnock, Ayrshire, for there was still a demand for the supply of spare parts for NBL-built steam locomotives and would be for some years to come. It took several years for the liquidation to be completed, and by 1968 all that remained of the gigantic conglomerate was the derelict hulk of the Hyde Park Works and the Administration Building in Flemington Street. As we have seen, this was to be used for a new purpose though still connected with the field of engineering.

Hyde Park Works and Atlas Works were eventually demolished; part of Queen's Park Works was taken over by the giant aluminium foil producing company Alcan. Alcan continues to employ the sons and daughters, and possibly grandchildren, of the men and women of the Queen's Park area, whose whole working lives had been devoted to the building of steam locomotives. A new generation in Springburn has never experienced the industry and bustle of the days when Springburn was one of the "Railway Towns" of Britain. Nor will young children be terrified by the sight of black faced men erupting in their thousands from the various works when the hooter sounds for the end of the working day. A strong affection for NBL still lives on in the minds of people like William Dewar. However, what was once a reality in which the people of Springburn and Queen's Park could take justifiable pride, the production of high quality steam locomotives, is now merely part of the long history of the city of Glasgow.

The North British Locomotive Company Administration Building, 110 Flemington Street, Springburn, Glasgow (now Glasgow North College of Engineering).

Perhaps some day a comparable new industry will rise to make Glasgow a world leader again, but it seems unlikely that there will be anything to rival the splendour of a brand new, brightly painted, steam locomotive emerging into the daylight for the first time from the Hyde Park or Queen's Park Works of the North British Locomotive Company.

NBL Locomotives Built for British Railway Companies

On 26th April 1903, the first order for a home railway was placed with the new NBL, from the Furness Railway which had been a regular customer of the old constituent companies. Built at the Atlas Works, the five locomotives of this order were of the 0-6-2T wheel arrangement. Until the Grouping in 1923, when the privately owned railway companies disappeared, most of the orders received from British railway companies were from Scotland, although quite a number were received from Ireland. By far the best customer of this period was the North British Railway, whose own Cowlairs Works was just a mile or so down the line from Hyde Park. Until 1923 the North British Railway, which had no connection with NBL, the one being a railway company and the other a locomotive building firm, placed a total of nineteen orders for 239 locomotives of varying types. The Highland Railway placed ten orders for 31 locomotives, including further examples of their "Ben" and "Castle" classes. The Caledonian Railway, another near neighbour, placed only four orders, but these totalled 42 locomotives. The Glasgow and South Western Railway, with eleven orders for 98 engines, and the Great North of Scotland Railway, with one order for 6, completed those from the Scottish railway companies. English and Welsh railway orders came also, but not as many from individual companies as from the major Scottish ones. Customers included the Barry Railway; the Midland and South Western Junction Railway; the Great Central Railway; the Furness Railway; the Maryport and Carlisle Railway; the North Eastern Railway; and the London, Tilbury and Southend Railway. Most of these orders were for small numbers of locomotives, which did not enable NBL to build the large numbers of standardised units for which their vast works could be used most effectively. This situation was remedied to some extent during World War I, when the Ministry of Munitions placed orders for a total of 396 2-8-0 locomotives for use in the movement of troops and munitions. From 1923 to 1948, and the formation of British Railways, the London, Midland and Scottish Railway, the London and North Eastern Railway, the Southern Railway, and even the Great Western Railway, which usually built its own locomotives, placed orders with NBL. These tended to be for larger numbers of engines, some of them not being completed until after the "Big Four" became British Railways.

Furness Railway No. 103. 18" 0-6-2T, with 5'1" coupled wheels. One of 5 built by the North British Locomotive Company in 1903-04.

With the nationalisation of the railways of Britain came an attempt to produce standardised locomotives which could be used across the entire country. The former "Big Four" had started this, but only within their own territories. While British Railways still kept their own types of express locomotives for use on the fast main line trains, they introduced new designs for slower routes and goods traffic which could be used anywhere. British Railways took over delivery of the last large orders which had been placed with the "Big Four" and were still in the process of completion, but did not place any new orders for their new designs for steam engines with NBL, so it could be said that the last orders for steam locomotives for the home railways were placed as far back as 1947. Orders placed after the Grouping until the completion of the last steam engine in 1952 were composed of 20 A1, later A3, 4-6-2s; 10 B17 "Sandringham" class 4-6-0s; 20 K3 2-6-0s; three orders for a total of 290 B1 4-6-0s; and 35 L1 2-6-4Ts, all for the London and North Eastern Railway. The Southern Railway ordered a total of thirty "King Arthur" class, 4-6-0s, so called because each locomotive was named after one of the knights of the legendary king, plus another order for fifteen 4-4-0s. The Great Western Railway placed only one order, which was split between Hyde Park and Queen's Park, for fifty 0-6-0Ts. The London, Midland and Scottish Railway orders included those for 4-4-0 compound locomotives; the "Royal Scots"; 4F class 0-6-0s; fifty "Jubilee" 4-6-0s; plus a variety of tank engines. As with World War I, World War II brought orders from the War Department, first for locomotives identical to the London, Midland and Scottish Railway's standard 8F class 2-8-0, and later for "Austerity" 2-8-0s and 2-10-0s, which NBL had a hand in designing. Strangely enough, not one of the most ubiquitous locomotives ever to run on British Railways, the Stanier designed class 5 4-6-0, of which 842 were built, was constructed by NBL.

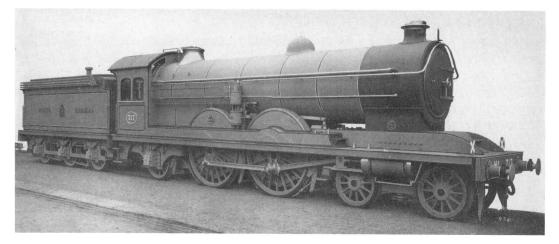

North Eastern Railway No. 717. Wilson Worsdell class 'Z' 15¹/₂" 3-cylinder 4-4-2, with 6'10" coupled wheels. One of 10 built by the North British Locomotive Company in 1911.

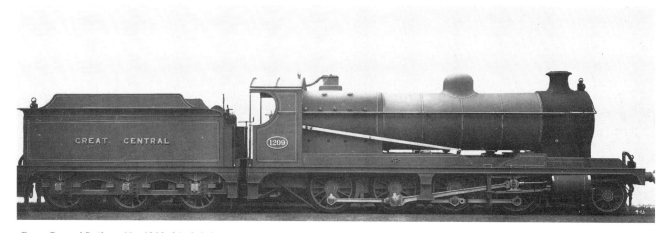

Great Central Railway No. 1209. 21" 2-8-0, with 4'8" coupled wheels. One of 50 built by the North British Locomotive Company in 1912-13.

(Top) Maryport & Carlisle Railway No. 18. 18" 0-6-0, with 5'1¹/₂" wheels. Built by the North British Locomotive Company in 1907.

(Middle) North British Railway No. 898 'Sir Walter Scott'. Reid 19" 'Scott' class 4-4-0, with 6'6" coupled wheels. One of 6 built by the North British Locomotive Company in 1909.

(Left) Glasgow & South Western Railway No. 545. Whitelegg 22" 4-6-4T, with 6'0" coupled wheels. One of 6 built by the North British Locomotive Company in 1921.

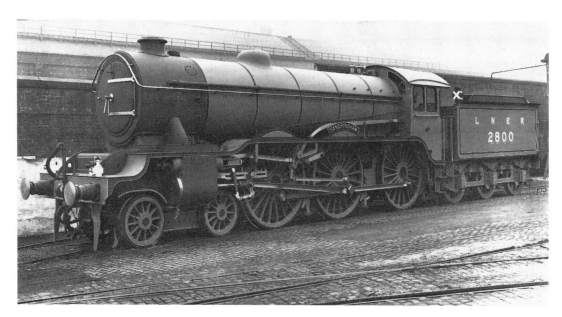

London & North Eastern Railway No. 2800 'Sandringham'. Gresley 17 1/2" 3-cylinder 'Sandringham' class 4-6-0, with 6'8" coupled wheels. One of 10 supplied by the North British Locomotive Company in 1928.

London & North Eastern Railway No. 2467. Gresley 18 1/2" class 'K3' 3-cylinder 2-6-0, with 5'8" coupled wheels. One of 20 built by the North British Locomotive Company in 1935.

London, Midland & Scottish Railway No. 2561. Stanier 19 ⁵/₈" 2-6-4T, with 5'9" coupled wheels.
One of 73 built by the North British Locomotive Company in 1936.

Ministry of Supply. 2-8-0. 100 built by the North British Locomotive Company in 1939-40.

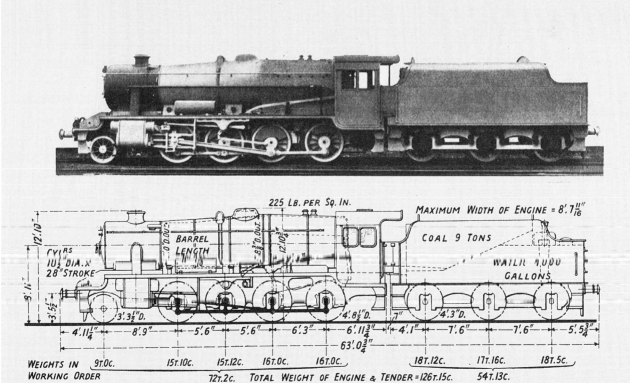

British Railways No. 90774. 'North British'. 19" 2-10-0, with 4'8½" coupled wheels. One of 100 originally built for the Ministry of Supply by the North British Locomotive Company in 1943. Riddles 'Austerity' locomotives. This view at Eastfield Shed, Glasgow, in June 1949. C L Kerr Collection, The Mitchell Library.

British Railways No. 61117. Thompson 20" class 'B1', 4-6-0, with 6'2" coupled wheels. One of 100 supplied by the North British Locomotive Company in 1946-47. Shown here ascending Cowlairs Bank, Glasgow, hauling the 'Queen of Scots Pullman' in July 1958. C L Kerr Collection, The Mitchell Library

British Railways No. 62010. Peppercorn 20" 'K1' 2-6-0, with 5'2" coupled wheels, undergoing steam tests in Queen's Park Works. One of 70 supplied by the North British Locomotive Company in 1949. Originally ordered by the London & North Eastern Railway in 1947.

The North British "Atlantics"

Built by NBL for the North British Railway under order number L175, fourteen of these 4-4-2 main line locomotives were completed and delivered in 1906. They were designed by William Paton Reid, no relation to the NBL Reids or their forebears, who was in charge at Cowlairs although he seems never to have been officially appointed locomotive superintendent. The "Atlantics" were spectacular in appearance with their high

London & North Eastern Railway No. 9876 'Waverley'. 'C11' class 4-4-2, with 6'9" coupled wheels. One of 14 originally supplied to the North British Railway by the North British Locomotive Company in 1906. Photographed outside Edinburgh Waverley Station in 1934. C L Kerr Collection, The Mitchell Library.

boilers. Each weighed 119 tons 16 cwt, and had 6' 9" driving wheels and outside cylinders 20"x 28" in size. They were the first North British Railway engines to be fitted with Belpaire fireboxes and carried North British Railway running numbers 868-881. The power of the "Atlantics" was intended to remove the necessity for double-heading on the "Waverley Route" and on the Edinburgh to Aberdeen expresses, but they proved too heavy for the track on these lines. Bridges would have to be strengthened and there was not a single turntable on the North British network which was big enough to turn them. After nearly two years in service some alterations were made to the engines which resolved their running problems, and a further six were ordered in 1911, this time from Robert Stephenson & Co. rather than NBL. A further two, with detail differences from the originals, were supplied by NBL in 1921. They all gave good service up to the 1930s when they were withdrawn at varying times. It was proposed that one be preserved for posterity, but it was scrapped during World War II.

North British Railway No. 509 'Duke of Rothesay'. 21" 4-4-2, with 6'9" coupled wheels. One of 2 supplied by the North British Locomotive Company in 1921.

*Two Gresley 'A1'
4-6-2s under
construction in the
Hyde Park Works
of the North
British Locomotive
Company.*

The London and North Eastern "Pacifics"

The 4-6-2, or "Pacific", wheel arrangement became predominant on the main lines of the London and North Eastern Railway. The class consisted of 78 locomotives in total, including the "Flying Scotsman", still preserved and one of the most famous locomotives in the world. Introduced on the former Great Northern Railway by Nigel Gresley in 1922, most were built at Doncaster, with the exception of twenty which were ordered from NBL in 1923. These twenty were built at Hyde Park Works under NBL order number L787, works numbers 23101-23120, and emerged as London and North Eastern Railway numbers 2563-2582. Like the others of their class, their driving wheels were 6' 8" in diameter, with bogie wheels and trailing wheels 3' 2" and 3' 8" in diameter respectively. The three cylinders, two outside and one inside, measured 20"x26". Boiler pressure was 180 pounds per square inch and weight in working order was 148 tons 15 cwt. By the 1920s steam locomotives had virtually reached the peak of their development. The twenty NBL "Pacifics", along with their English-built counterparts, having received various modifications, served on the King's Cross to London expresses and elsewhere until the demise of steam on British Railways in the 1960s. They were only surpassed in performance by the later A4 "Pacifics", one of which, number 4468 "Mallard", achieved the world speed record of 126 miles per hour on 3rd July 1938.

London & North Eastern Railway No. 2563 'William Whitelaw'. Gresley 3-cylinder 4-6-2, with coupled wheels. One of 20 supplied by the North British Locomotive Company in 1924. Originally 'A1', later 'A3' class.

The "Royal Scots"

For a time after World War I, the London, Midland and Scottish Railway suffered a dearth of high quality main line express passenger locomotives. There were various reasons for this, one of them being that the War precluded anything other than the maintenance of the existing fleet of locomotives. In addition, the men in charge of the railway from its inception in 1923 were mostly from the old Midland Railway, where the smallish mainline locomotives were adequate for that system, but not for hauling heavy trains over the extended territory of the new railway. Ex-Midland Railway, ex-London and North Western Railway, and ex-Lancashire and Yorkshire Railway locomotives, while good for what they were originally intended, were too old, or were simply not powerful enough for their new roles. There was also a lack of design skill amongst their engineers. Changes to the London, Midland and Scottish Railway board in 1925 brought about some action. The board now began to examine the main-line locomotive stock of the other three members of the "Big Four", and found that their own was inferior. The chief mechanical engineer of the London, Midland and Scottish, Henry Fowler, was then instructed to draw up designs for a new type of more powerful locomotive. The design for a three-cylinder, high boiler pressure, 4-6-0 was passed to the North British Locomotive Company in 1926, with the requirement that 50 of the locomotives were to be ready for the London, Midland and Scottish summer traffic of 1927. The railway's own works did not have the capacity to build such locomotives in a short space of time, whereas NBL's vast resources were ideal. The designs did not include anything like the full details required for the finished product. The drawing office staff at NBL ironed out these problems and construction of the "Royal Scot" class began.

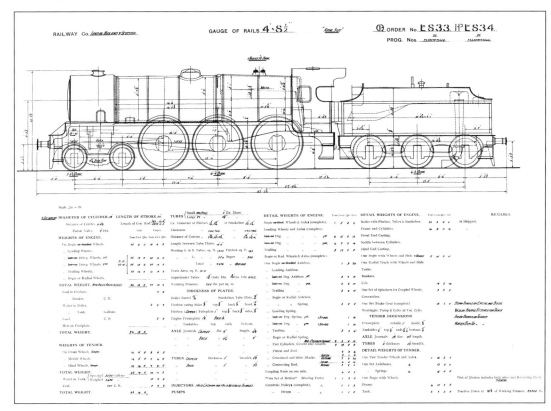

Weight diagram of 'Royal Scot' class.

Polmadie Engine Shed, Glasgow, in summer 1928, showing 'Royal Scot' class Nos. 6132, 6128 and 6127. R B Haddon Collection, The Mitchell Library.

*'Royal Scot' class 6133 disguised as 6100 'Royal Scot' for the North British Locomotive Company's
official photograph. The number 6133 is stamped on the union link.*

The order for 50 was divided into two parts with NBL order L833, works numbers 23595
-23619, LMSR running numbers 6100-6124 being built at Queen's Park Works, and order
L834, works numbers 23620-23644, LMSR nos. 6125-6149, going to Hyde Park. It was decided
that one engine should be completed in the shortest possible time with the others to follow.
LMSR no. 6100, named "Royal Scot", was duly completed and dispatched to the railway on
14th July 1927, so quickly that NBL did not even have time to photograph the prototype for
their official archives. Early photographs of the locomotive in service depict it without
nameplates, which were retained by NBL until they could take the required photographs. At
least three others of the class were disguised to look like 6100 for this purpose. NBL made
very little profit on the order in spite of all the trouble taken with the designs.

The completed locomotives weighed 127.85 tons in working order; each had three cylinders
of size 18"x 26", coupled wheel diameter of 6' 9", and a boiler pressure of 250 pounds per
square inch. At first they were put into service in different parts of the LMSR, but from 26th
September 1927 they were allocated to haul the London to Glasgow express trains the 300
miles non-stop from Euston to Carlisle, the longest non-stop run in the world at the time.
Another "Scot" then took over for the run from Carlisle to Glasgow. For this purpose several
"Scots" were allocated to the LMSR depot at Polmadie in Glasgow, a short distance from
NBL's Queen's Park Works where the class had been born. The Glasgow-built "Scots" continued
to give sterling service up to the 1940s and in some cases the 1950s, with each one being
eventually rebuilt with a tapered boiler and other modifications. In this condition they lasted
until the 1960s when British Railways were phasing out steam in favour of diesel and electric
locomotives.

London, Midland & Scottish Railway No. 6128 on express near Symington shortly after delivery by the North British Locomotive Company.

Another NBL-built locomotive which finished up as a rebuilt "Royal Scot" was the experimental LMS no. 6399 "Fury", completed under NBL order L858, works number 23890, in 1929. With the same frames, wheel arrangement and cab as an original NBL "Scot", what differed about "Fury" was its boiler, which was of triple pressure. The ordinary boiler pressure was the same 250 pounds per square inch of the conventional "Scot", but an additional steel drum had a pressure of 900 pounds per square inch, with the firebox water tubes having a pressure varying from 1,400 to 1,800 pounds per square inch. The purpose of this experimental engine was to examine methods of improving thermal efficiency in large steam locomotives. After extensive tests at Hyde Park Works, which were deemed successful, the locomotive was put on an extended run on 10th February 1930. All went well until the train was entering Carstairs Station, when one of the 1,800 per square inch tubes ruptured, killing an inspector and seriously injuring the fireman. Five years later "Fury" was rebuilt as an ordinary "Scot" and renamed "British Legion" with the running number 6170. In this format it survived until 1st December 1962.

London, Midland & Scottish railway experimental 4-6-0 'Fury'. Shown here on test prior to delivery in 1929.

The "Scotch Arthurs"

The formation of the Southern Railway in 1923 as one of the "Big Four" brought about the same kind of problems with locomotive stock as those encountered by the London, Midland and Scottish Railway at its induction. The former independent railway companies all had adequate, if in some cases ageing, locomotives suited to their own needs. The new management of the Southern Railway therefore were looking for ways to spruce up the new railway's image. One of the ideas put forward which was hoped to capture the public's imagination was the naming of a new class of locomotive after the mythic heroes of Camelot, and so the "King Arthur" class was born. The original examples of the class were built at Eastleigh Works, but it was not until the superheated version was supplied from NBL that they became most successful. Twenty of these upgraded "Arthurs" were ordered from NBL in 1924, with a further order for ten in 1925. All were built at Hyde Park, hence their nickname "Scotch Arthurs". The first batch was ordered under NBL order L800, working numbers 23209-23232 and Southern Railway running numbers 763-782, with the second batch being order L803, works numbers 23279-23288, running numbers 783-792. Wheel arrangement was 4-6-0, outside cylinder size 20½"x 28", driving-wheel diameter was 6' 7", and the bogie wheels 3' 7" in diameter. Boiling pressure was 200 pounds per square inch and overall weight in working order 138½ tons. The locomotive depicted in the official NBL works photograph, no. 767 "Sir Valence", was originally intended to be named "Sir Mordred". The name was altered when it was remembered that Mordred was the villain of the Arthurian legends, and it was deemed unsuitable to have a locomotive named after him.

Southern Railway No. 767 'Sir Valence'. Maunsell 20½" 'King Arthur' class 4-6-0, with 6'7" driving wheels. One of 30 built by the North British Locomotive Company in 1925.

After delivery the "Scotch Arthurs" hauled the boat trains from London to the English Channel ports and also the expresses to Bournemouth. They were reliable, had more than enough power and brought a touch of glamour to the locomotive stock of the Southern Railway. The entire class progressed into British Railways in 1948, and in most cases lasted until the early 1960s when the Southern Region began to phase out steam in favour of diesel and electric powered locomotives.

The "Jubilees"

As the 1930s progressed, one of the most famous steam locomotive designers of all became Locomotive Superintendent on the London, Midland and Scottish Railway. This was William, later Sir William, Stanier. If there was a lack of designing skill on the LMSR when it first came into being Stanier more than made up for the earlier inadequacies. His new designs were to proliferate in the LMSR, and the "Jubilees" were one of them. The engines received their class name as a tribute to King George V, whose silver jubilee as king had been reached in 1933. Every locomotive in the class was named after a country, state or province in the British Empire. Fifty examples of these locomotives were built by NBL, under their order number L885, works numbers 24115-24164, LMSR running numbers 5557-5606, with 25 being built per works. They were of 4-6-0 wheel arrangement, with three cylinders, two outside and one inside, measuring 17"x 26", coupled wheel diameter 6' 9", boiler pressure of 225 pounds per square inch, and a weight in full working order of 79½ tons, not including tender weight. All were fitted with superheaters, although these were replaced with newer ones during the life of the locomotives. They had taper boilers, similar to those with which the "Royal Scots" were fitted when their original boilers were replaced. The locomotives were very successful, being used to haul many important trains all over the LMSR tracks. Most of them survived up to the demise of steam, with two of the NBL built batch nos. 5593 "Kolhapur" and 5596 "Bahamas", being restored, and still hauling trains on special occasions, some 63 years after their construction.

London, Midland & Scottish Railway No. 5573. Stanier 17" 3 cylinder "Jubilee" class 4-6-0, with 6'9" coupled wheels. One of 50 built by the North British Locomotive Company in 1934.

Industrial Locomotives

So far examination has been made of some of the better known classes of locomotive built by NBL. In addition to express locomotives, the company and its three constituents built many different types of freight and shunting locomotives for the railways of Britain. These locomotives, of both tender and tank design, were the true workhorses of the railway networks, moving the products of the nation without much attention being paid to them by the general public. They were for the most part unglamorous in their appearance, their purpose being to haul large loads consistently and efficiently at much slower speeds than the elite passenger engines. Many of them were utilised at night, moving ponderously along the main lines with massive loads of coal or other materials, being shunted off the main lines when a passenger express was due to come roaring through at a speed sometimes in excess of 70 miles per hour. Often freight trains could take the same number of days to travel the length of the country as a fast express would take hours. Many of the smaller tender engines and tank locomotives spent their entire existence on meandering branch lines with a stop at every station. But these were no less important to the communities they served than their more impressive counterparts which moved the latest carriages at high speeds between cities. Rural services were not at all profitable to the railway companies, except in the heyday of the railways, and with the advent of motor cars and lorries many of these lines were closed. Construction of such steam locomotives provided a great deal of income over the years to the commercial locomotive builders such as NBL and its predecessors.

Another type of customer was the large industrial manufacturer, who needed steam locomotives to haul materials and finished products within the confines of his own premises. Many iron and steel works, producers of heavy machinery, coal mines and even breweries required small reliable engines which could work consistently with little maintenance for a great number of years. Often these locomotives were built to run on narrow gauge track, for example 2' 0" compared with the 4' 8½" of the public railways, but many had to be used to send goods out all over the country and therefore were of standard gauge. Most of these locomotives were of 0-4-0 or 0-6-0 wheel arrangement, and were usually tank rather than tender engines, not required to carry large amounts of coal or water as they did not have to travel long distances from a source of supply. These locomotives were small and orders were at the most usually for one or two units. Glasgow builders supplied large numbers of this type of engine to a variety of customers. Neilson & Co. built what could be called a standard design of tank locomotive which was instantly recognisable as a Neilson product. The saddle tank, located on top of the boiler, wrapped around it as it were, resembled a grand piano in shape, so that the locomotives became known as "Piano tanks". At one time these locomotives were in such demand that Neilson & Co. built some for stock, and a prospective customer could buy one off the shelf. Dübs & Co. also produced an extremely useful type of industrial locomotive, usually of 0-4-0 wheel arrangement, with the tanks mounted on each side of the boiler rather than on top of it. These locomotives had a crane mounted on specially constructed frames on top of the boiler which could lift weights of up to five tons or more. The cranes were able to swivel sideways in any direction so that heavy objects could be lifted from the ground on to wagons for transportation, or used in a variety of different ways. This made the locomotive much more useful than a conventional one, so Dübs & Co. patented the idea.

12" 0-4-0T engine built by Neilson & Co. for the Hockley Hall & Whateley Collieries in 1888.

In the early days when he was establishing his firm, Walter Neilson commented that he might never have succeeded had it not been for the orders he received from Scottish public railway companies. He must also have been thankful for the orders the industrial companies placed with him, for they were considerable. Many were from local companies who probably gave the new firm a try purely because it was local and they did not wish to incur expensive transportation costs. Satisfied with their initial engines, many of them came back for others. Examples of local industrial companies who placed orders with Neilson & Co. include William Baird of Gartsherrie, who ordered a total of seven locomotives during the early years; the Coltness Iron Co.; Dalmellington Iron; the Dixon & Govan Colliery; Eglinton Iron; Glasgow Iron; Glengarnock Iron; the Monklands Iron Co., who ordered ten engines all told; Shotts Iron; and Summerlee Iron. Other, more distantly located, Scottish customers included Elgin Collieries and the Forth Iron Co. Even in those early days, Neilson & Co., had several orders from English companies and a surprising number from Welsh industrial concerns, far more than he was able to get from the passenger railway companies. His biggest English customer was the Furness Mining Co., who ordered six locomotives at different times, with the Ebbw Vale Co. of Wales topping that with eight. Other early Welsh orders came from Dowlairs Iron; Pontypool Iron; and the Rhos Colliery. These are only a selection of the orders received from industrial customers. Comparison with those received from railway companies in this early period shows that industrial manufacturing company orders were by far the more numerous, with numbers of engines ordered by both types of customer being about equal. Following Walter Montgomerie Neilson's decision to concentrate purely on the manufacture of steam locomotives, orders for industrial locomotives continued to roll in. Even after his departure from the firm the Chartered Gas Company, Neilson & Co.'s best industrial customer, placed no less than twenty-four separate orders. The faithful William Baird & Co. came second with a further fifteen orders. Neilson also filled six orders for crane locomotives, presumably all under the terms dictated by Dübs' patents.

Dübs & Co. also received a fair number of orders from industrial customers including nine from the Steel Company of Scotland, their best industrial customer. Many of their customers were different firms from those who ordered from Neilson, but there was a certain amount of overlap. A locomotive supplied under Dübs' order E1071 may still be in existence, if anyone is brave enough to go searching for it. This engine was supplied to the Easdale Slate Co., of Easdale, Argyll, and was used for hauling wagons of slate from the quarries. Practically the entire centuries-old Easdale slate industry was wiped out in one night during a violent storm on 22nd November 1881 when the sea flooded the quarries which extended under it. The locomotive is said to have fallen into the bottom of the quarry when the track underneath it collapsed during this storm. It could still be there, buried under tons of slate.

14" 0-4-0T engine built by Neilson & Co. for the Singer Manufacturing Company in 1896.

10" 0-4-0T crane locomotive built by Dübs & Co. for stock in 1868.

Glasgow Corporation Gas No. 4. 6" 0-4-0T, with 1'8" driving wheels. One of 5 built by Sharp,Stewart & Co. in 1893.

The Clyde Locomotive Company received only one order from a British industrial firm during its brief existence. This was from the Eglinton Iron Co. who had ordered earlier engines from Neilson. Following Sharp, Stewart & Co.'s move to Glasgow, they received some orders but not as many as they had in Manchester, and some of the Glasgow orders were from industrial customers who had previously dealt with them in England. There are however, a couple of instances which clearly illustrate the problems of competition between the three Glasgow firms. Mention has already been made of the numbers of orders Neilson & Co. received from William Baird & Co., but this could have been even more, for Dübs & Co. obtained two, and Sharp, Stewart & Co. received two, although these latter two may have been placed out of loyalty to Walter Montgomerie Neilson, now a partner in Sharp, Stewart. The other example concerns Glasgow Corporation Gas. All three of the NBL constituent firms built locomotives for them within a twenty year period. If there had been only one company in Glasgow perhaps it would have received all the orders. The first locomotives supplied by a Glasgow locomotive builder to Glasgow Corporation Gas were three 0-4-0Ts, supplied under Dübs order E1234, works numbers 1234-1236, running numbers 1-3. A repeat order for no. 4 was placed in 1884. Neilson & Co. supplied a total of three 0-4-0Ts also, under two orders E751 and E899 placed in 1895 and 1902 respectively. Sharp, Stewart & Co. filled orders for a total of twelve locomotives under orders E1023, E1034, and E1101, placed in 1893 for the first two and 1896 for the last.

Not all the locomotives were the same as Glasgow Corporation Gas operated two railway systems. The first was of standard gauge which was reflected in the size of the locomotives. Dübs order E1234 was built for this system with the locomotives weighing twenty tons, having a capacity for 500 gallons of water and space for 24 cubic feet of coal. Driving wheel diameter was 3' 0", cylinder size 12"x 20" and boiler pressure 130 pounds per square inch. Comparison of the Dübs engines with those of Sharp, Stewart order E1023, for locomotives of 2' 0" gauge reveals what must have been five of the smallest working locomotives ever built. The locomotives had a wheelbase of 2' 7", cylinders of size 6" x 9" and driving wheel diameter of 1' 8". Compared with the 500 gallons of the standard gauge locomotives, the 2' 0" ones had a tank located under the smoke-box which when full, held twenty gallons of water. Both of these water capacities pale into insignificance when compared with the 4,000 gallons carried in the tender of a "Royal Scot" or the 5,000 gallons of an A3, inside which the entire 2' 0" Glasgow Corporation Gas engines could have been sunk without even being noticed. The diminutive 0-4-0Ts were designed for use inside the Gasworks, and had to run in areas where there was limited height clearance. Because of this Glasgow Corporation Gas employed equally diminutive men to drive the locomotives. Their lack of height would protect them while they stood on the footplates as the locomotives moved under the projections of overhead machinery.

Many customers for industrial locomotives who had purchased from the three constituent firms continued to buy from NBL after its formation. The range and variety of such locomotives was wide, but advancing technology was as evident in industrial locomotives as in the types bought by the railway companies.

Coltness Iron Company No. 3. 18" 0-6-0T, with 4'3" wheels built by the North British Locomotive Company in 1913.

Diesel Locomotives

By the time NBL seriously attempted to make inroads into the burgeoning diesel locomotive market, British Railways had been formed and was, therefore, the only public railway system in Britain from which NBL could hope to attract orders. By then much of the market had been captured by firms like English Electric and Sulzer. An order for a single diesel locomotive was received from the London, Midland and Scottish Railway in late 1947 but was not completed until British Railways days. The specification for this locomotive, which became British Railways no. 10800, was submitted to NBL by the LMSR. This would account for the fact that power from the diesel engine was transmitted to the driving wheels by electric transmission, the method preferred by British Railways, whereas the majority of mainline diesels later supplied to British Railways by NBL had their preferred type of transmission, diesel hydraulic. 10800 was an 827 horsepower Bo-Bo locomotive, the wheel arrangement so-called because it had a single bogie at each end containing four wheels of diameter 3' 6". The diesel power unit was a 16-cylinder Davey Paxman engine and the electrical equipment was supplied by British Thomson Houston. The locomotive was designed for usage on branch lines and for hauling mid-range freight trains. Another order for ten similar locomotives with modifications, but also with diesel-electric transmission, was placed with NBL in 1955. They were delivered in 1958, almost a year behind schedule.

The 2,000 horse power "Warship" class, of which the first five prototypes were dispatched from NBL in 1958, were the most powerful diesel locomotives of their day. The class was so called as each example was named after a famous warship. British Railways running numbers were D600-D604 and the locomotives originally ran on the Western Region express trains from Paddington Station in London as far west as Cornwall. They were powered by two 1,000 brake horse power diesel units of the NBL/MAN 12 cylinder L12V 18/21S variety with the hydraulic transmission being Voith-North British type L306r. To produce the required power, these MAN engines had to run at a very high speed. Difficulties were encountered with the various types of these engines when it came to transmitting the power they produced to the Voith transmission systems to pass to the wheels. Because these systems were hydraulic they had to be operated inside an oil-filled container to cut down on excessive wear of the moving parts.

British Railways No. D600 'Active'. A1A-A1A 'Warship' class Type 4. One of five built by the North British Locomotive Company in 1958.

The oil-baths proved prone to leakage due to the pressure built up by the moving parts causing NBL problems with their diesel hydraulic locomotives; but the company was committed to this and could not change without incurring a great deal of expense. The high-speed MAN engines also tended to wear more quickly than the slower turning equivalent being applied by NBL's competitors. No more of this type of "Warship" were ever built, although the name was reused for an entirely different design a few years later. These engines differed from D600-D604 in that they had bulbous ends rather than square ones. The first thirty-three were built by British Railways themselves,

British Railways No. D8402. Bo Bo Type 1. One of 10 delivered by the North British Locomotive Company in 1958.

but a second batch of thirty-three was ordered from NBL towards the end of 1958. The power units and other component parts in these thirty-three locomotives were similar to those of D600-D604, and consequently the engines had the same kind of problems. Their NBL/MAN engines were of 1,100 brake horse power rather than the 1,000 of the earlier series but transmission units were the same.

Other lower powered locomotives, fairly similar in appearance to the original "Warships", were ordered by the Western Region and appeared in 1959. Powered by a single NBL/MAN L12V18 diesel, no less than fifty-eight of these locomotives were built, their running numbers being D6300-D6357. Similar engines, nos. D6100-D6157, but with 1,100 hp. diesel engines rather than 1,000, were built by NBL for use in the Scottish Region. Their major difference was General Electric Company diesel-electric transmission units rather than Voith diesel-hydraulic. Although their transmission method was different, the Scottish locomotives still had problems with the high-speed power units and were never truly successful. Some were eventually re-engined with a non-NBL manufactured power unit. This marked the end of the production of diesel locomotives by NBL for British Railways. It speaks volumes that, when diesel locomotives began to be withdrawn from service, those which NBL built were the first to go, in some cases after a life of only a few years. Contributing factors were the continual maintenance problems, plus the excessive noise which the high-speed power units produced. NBL also filled a few orders for small diesel shunters for British Railways, and these proved effective, but difficulties with main line diesel locomotives proved to be the foremost cause of the firm's closure. This occurred a mere two years after the delivery of the last main line diesel locomotives. Preceding this they had received a few small orders from industrial British companies for diesel locomotives similar to the shunters supplied to British Railways.

Electric Locomotives

Ten electric locomotives were built for British Railways at Hyde Park Works, to an order placed in February 1957. NBL works numbers were 27793-27802, British Railways running numbers E3036-E3045, and the locomotives were built in conjunction with the General Electric Company. These were later reclassified and renumbered 84001-84010. They were constructed for the purpose of running on the electrified Manchester to Crewe line, and were capable of speeds of 100 miles per hour. Unfortunately, the series were plagued with problems from the time they entered service and required much modification. Even then they lasted only until the late 1970s before being withdrawn from service.

British Railways No. D6303. B-B Type 2. One of 58 built by the North British Locomotive Company in 1959.

Other Glasgow Locomotive Builders

From the time of Neilson's first venture into locomotive building until the demise of the mammoth North British Locomotive Company in 1962, a few other firms, mostly on a small scale, had built locomotives in Glasgow. One of these could match NBL in size but not in the building of steam locomotives, which was only a small part of its activities. This was William Beardmore & Co. Ltd., of Dalmuir and Parkhead. This company could trace its origins back to 1835 and went on to become one of the largest heavy engineering firms of its time. It concentrated on filling the demands for steel and machinery which came from the large Glasgow shipyards and did not enter locomotive building until 1920, continuing till 1931. Most of its locomotives went overseas but for the railways of Britain the company built twenty 4-6-0 locomotives for the Great Eastern Railway in 1920; ninety "Prince of Wales" class 4-6-0s for the London and North Western Railway in 1920-1921; one 4-6-0 and ninety 0-6-0Ts for the London, Midland and Scottish Railway in 1924 and 1927 respectively; and twenty 0-6-2Ts for the London and North Eastern Railway in 1927. All the aforementioned were built at Beardmore's Dalmuir premises which, following the end of World War I, had been converted from an arms factory to a locomotive erecting shop. For eleven or so years when Beardmore built steam locomotives, they had facilities to match the output of NBL, which must have given that company cause for concern.

Other firms which built locomotives in Glasgow were much smaller, with most of their output being early locomotives. They included Thomas Edington & Sons, of the Phoenix Iron Works, an early builder who completed a total output of four 2-2-2s for the Glasgow, Paisley, Kilmarnock and Ayr Railway in 1840-1841; McHendrick and Ball who were thought to have built one locomotive in 1878; the St. Rollox Foundry Company, where Walter Montgomerie Neilson served part of his apprenticeship, built four locomotives for the Garnkirk and Glasgow

British Railways No. 61555. Holden 20" class B12 4-6-0, with 6'6" coupled wheels. One of 20 originally built for the Great Eastern Railway by William Beardmore & Co. in 1920-21. C L Kerr Collection, The Mitchell Library.

Railway between 1835 and 1840; and Stark & Fulton who built nine 2-2-0s between 1839 and 1841 and a single 2-2-2 in 1849. One later firm was the Glasgow Railway Engineering Co., owned by Dugald Drummond, a man whose entire life had been spent in the services of various major railway companies, including the Caledonian and the North British. His firm, located at Helen Street, Govan, was founded in 1891, and built a number of locomotives over the next ten years, including seven narrow gauge 0-4-0WTs for Glasgow Corporation Gas. The company then seems to have discontinued the construction of steam locomotives, but continued to manufacture, among other things, railway wheels and axles.

Cowlairs Works

With the opening of the Edinburgh and Glasgow Railway in 1842, a railway workshop was built in the Cowlairs area of Glasgow. Originally intended for the repair of that railway's own locomotives, in 1844 it built its first two complete locomotives for the operation of the Cowlairs Incline. In 1865 the Edinburgh and Glasgow Railway became part of the North British Railway and the following year Cowlairs became the main works of that railway. Up to the North British Railway's disappearance into the London and North Eastern Railway as part of the Grouping in 1923, Cowlairs Works had produced about 850 locomotives. They were all for the use of the railway to which it belonged, and the site had grown to almost 167 acres in size. No locomotives were built after 1923, but repair and maintenance work carried on, even into British Railways and the eventual replacement of the steam locomotive. The works finally closed in 1968, with outstanding contracts being transferred to nearby St. Rollox. During its Edinburgh and Glasgow and North British Railway days, Cowlairs produced some of the finest locomotives ever to run on a Scottish railway, including the "Scott" and "Glen" 4-4-0s. These were named after characters in the novels of Sir Walter Scott and Scottish glens respectively. Many prominent railway engineers figured in the history of Cowlairs, including Dugald Drummond, who was locomotive superintendent of the North British from 1875 until 1882.

St. Rollox Works

Much smaller than Cowlairs, occupying fifteen acres, St. Rollox Works was to the Caledonian Railway what Cowlairs was to the North British, a railway company workshop. The works were built in 1853 for the repair and maintenance of Caledonian Railway stock, and produced

British Railways No. 62487 'Glen Arklet'. Reid North British Railway 'Glen' class 4-4-0, with 6'0" coupled wheels. Design introduced in 1913, with this example being built at Cowlairs Works in 1920. Photographed at Edinburgh Waverley Station in April 1949. C L Kerr Collection, The Mitchell Library.

British Railways Nos. 62432 'Quentin Durward' and 62428 'The Talisman'. Reid North British Railway 'Scott' class 4-4-0s, with 6'6" coupled wheels. Design introduced 1912, with both these examples being built at Cowlairs Works in 1914. Photographed at Hawick in August 1952. C L Kerr Collection, The Mitchell Library.

their first new locomotive in 1854. Until it was swallowed up in 1923 by the London, Midland and Scottish Railway, the works produced numerous new types of locomotives for the Caledonian, including the various versions of the "Dunalastair" 4-4-0s and the "Cardean" express 4-6-0s. In 1882 Dugald Drummond left the North British Railway for the post of locomotive superintendent on the Caledonian where he remained until 1890. Whilst with the Caledonian he introduced several highly successful 4-4-0 designs, some of which remained in service with British Railways until the early 1960s. He was not, however, responsible for building the "Dunalastairs", the first of which did not appear until 1896. These were designed by the then locomotive superintendent John Farquharson McIntosh, but Drummond certainly paved the way for them.

Locomotive construction at St. Rollox ended in 1928, but repair work was to continue for many years with the works becoming the main British Railways Scottish works in 1968. In January 1970 it became part of British Rail Engineering Ltd.; the name was changed to the Glasgow Works in 1972. In 1987 the works became part of British Rail Maintenance Ltd. situated off Springburn Road, less than a mile to the east of the Royal Infirmary. The previous St. Rollox Works if somewhat reduced in size, became the last bastion of the railway industry which had been the very life and soul of Springburn for over one hundred and fifty years. At their peak, both Cowlairs and St. Rollox had each employed thousands of men in railway work, alongside the thousands employed by the Springburn based works of the North British Locomotive Company. Springburn was a railway town within the city of Glasgow, and it would be nigh impossible to establish the true number of Glasgow citizens who owed their livelihood to the prosperity of the Glasgow railway industry, not only in Springburn, but also in Queen's Park. The age of the steam locomotive has truly gone from Glasgow, as it has elsewhere, but Glasgow's contribution to the industry and to the locomotive stock of the railways of Britain will never be surpassed.

London, Midland & Scottish Railway No. 14803. Ex-Caledonian Railway No. 959. Pickersgill 3-cylinder '956' class 4-6-0, with 6'1" coupled wheels. One of 4 built at St. Rollox Works in 1921. Photographed near Elvanfoot on a goods train in 1927. R B Haddon Collection, The Mitchell Library.

The Records

All the photographic records, company order books etc., of NBL and the three constituent companies, which were in the company's possession at the time of its closure were passed to the Mitchell Library, North Street, Glasgow, G3 7DN, for permanent conservation. First came all photographs prior to 1939, donated to the library in 1965, with those from 1939 to 1962 following shortly afterwards. The second batch were originally passed on to Andrew Barclay, Sons, & Co., of Kilmarnock, as a goodwill gesture. The basic collection consists of about 9,000 glass negatives of various sizes, with a similar number of photographs. From the early days up to about 1910, each order for locomotives was represented by one photograph, no matter how many locomotives may have comprised the total order. This single print was usually a formally posed side view with the background masked out. Later, in addition to the masked side view, there were diagonal views, both masked and unmasked, others of the front and rear of locomotives, and if the locomotives were tender engines, views of the cab end and of the front of the tender. Most of the negatives for these views are 16" x 12" and are made of glass. Dating from 1925 there are a variety of smaller glass plate negatives, of whole plate, half plate, or quarter plate size, which depict scenes of workshop interiors with locomotives under construction. Some also show locomotives in transit through the streets of Glasgow, being loaded aboard ships at Glasgow docks, and technical views of details of the more significant locomotives. All the diesel negatives are of whole plate size or smaller.

The photographic representation of Neilson & Co. goes back to 1864, and in the case of Dübs & Co. and the Clyde Locomotive Co., to their earliest locomotives. Sharp, Stewart & Co. products are comprehensively covered from 1888, but there are very few photographs from their Manchester period. There are other gaps in the collection, particularly relating to repeat orders for identical locomotives. Photographs have been printed of all negatives from which no prints had been made, and a virtually complete set of photographs is now available in the library for reference purposes. These are arranged by company order number, the numbers being traced from the various company works lists.

In addition to the photographs and negatives, the collection houses a number of important volumes relating to the locomotives of the various firms. There is a comprehensive collection of order books, works lists and drawing office registers, covering the complete output of all the companies. The only major works missing are the order books covering the years 1866-1887 for Sharp, Stewart & Co., although details of their products for this period can be compiled from other sources. A most important source of information is a set of fifteen weight diagram books covering Neilson & Co.'s. output from 1864 onwards, plus the steam locomotives built by NBL. Another important volume is the one which records the steaming and delivery dates of locomotives completed between 1928 and 1951. There are also two volumes containing diagrams of projected Neilson locomotive designs which were never executed.

At present the Mitchell Library collection forms part of the stock of the History and Glasgow Department. It is not on view to the general public although items from it can be requested for perusal. It is advised that persons requiring information from the collection should apply in writing well in advance of any proposed visit. Members of the public writing to make such an appointment or with any enquiry relating to the records should address correspondence to the Director.

Locomotive drawings, other than weight diagrams, are not part of the Mitchell Library collection. Most general arrangement drawings, particularly for the locomotives of NBL from 1903 onwards, are in the possession of the Archives Department, University of Glasgow, Glasgow, G12 8QQ, and any enquiries relating to them should be made to that address. Constituent company drawings are held by the National Railway Museum, York.

Springburn Museum

At 179 Ayr Street, Springburn, within a stone's throw of where the main gates of Hyde Park Works were located, stands Glasgow City Libraries and Archives Department's Springburn Library. The library was built on ground donated to the City of Glasgow by the NBL Reid family for that purpose. For many years the citizens of Springburn could borrow both fiction and non-fiction from the library or visit it to read the current newspapers. The Springburn Library had a special responsibility to reflect the local railway activities and stocked more books connected with railways than any other lending library in the city.

At the end of 1985 alterations were made to the reading room of Springburn Library turning it into a museum to house and preserve artefacts and information concerning all aspects of the history of Springburn. It opened in 1986 and in the following year its first special major exhibition depicted the prominence of the railway within the community. Activities by the Springburn Museum expanded to take in all aspects of life in the district which depended so much on the railway industry for its survival. In its recent past the Museum has extended its exhibition activities, putting on as many as six per year. Plans were put forward for the building of additional exhibition halls on the site of the derelict Hyde Park Works. The centrepiece was to have been a huge Garratt locomotive which had been brought back from South African Railways. This proposal fell through owing to lack of funding, with the locomotive now in the open air museum at Summerlee, where it is likely to remain.

Springburn Museum is administered by a trust, among whose members is William Dewar. In the 1997-1998 budget allocations Glasgow City Council, who were facing severe cutbacks in all aspects of their finance, cut their grant to Springburn Museum by fifty per cent. This has forced the Museum to close on Mondays, and the working hours of the staff have also had to be reduced. Still Springburn Museum carries on, receiving visitors from all over the world, many of whom are expatriate Scots whose forebears built the locomotives or were engaged in the other railway activities of Springburn. Hopefully Springburn Museum will manage to obtain extra funding from other sources and return to its full operation. More than anywhere else the museum reflects the railway era of Springburn which is gone, never to return. Situated in the area which was once one of the greatest railway communities ever known, this last reminder of what Springburn once was, the builder of locomotives for Britain and the World, should never be allowed to disappear.

Members of Springburn Museum Trust examine an album of Old Springburn photos during an exhibition opening, 1996. Courtesy of Springburn Museum.

Chronology

1722 - Tranent to Cockenzie wooden-railed wagonway built.

1816 - Henry Dübs born.

1819 - Walter Montgomerie Neilson born.

1823 - James Reid born.

1831 - First locomotives, for the Monkland and Kirkintilloch Railway, built by Murdoch, Aitken & Co.

1833 - Sharp, Roberts & Co., (later Sharp, Stewart & Co.) of Manchester built their first locomotive.

1836 - Neilson & Mitchell founded in Hyde Park Street, Finnieston, Glasgow.

1842 - Cowlairs Works built.

1843 - First Neilson locomotives for a Scottish railway built, for the Garnkirk and Glasgow Railway.

1845 - Finnieston Street Foundry opened.

1852 - James Reid appointed as Works Manager of Neilson & Co.

1853 - St Rollox Works built.

1858 - James Reid replaced by Henry Dübs.

1862 - Transfer of Neilson & Co. Works from Finnieston Street to Springburn.

1863 - Henry Dübs left to set up Glasgow Locomotive Works. Replaced by James Reid.

1876 - Reid in complete control of Neilson & Co. Dübs died.

1884 - Neilson set up Clyde Locomotive Company in Springburn.

1888 - Neilson sold the Clyde Locomotive Company to Sharp, Stewart & Co. Works renamed the Atlas Works.

1889 - Neilson died.

1894 - Reid died.

1898 - Neilson & Co. became Neilson, Reid & Co. with Hugh Reid as senior partner.

1902 - Neilson, Reid & Co. donated land for Springburn Library.

1903 - North British Locomotive Company formed by amalgamation of Neilson, Reid & Co.; Dübs & Co.; and Sharp, Stewart & Co.

1909 - Administration Building (now Glasgow North College) opened.

1914 - Boom caused by World War I.

1920 - Locomotive building begun by William Beardmore & Co.

1923 - Formation of the Grouping. Disappearance of privately owned railway companies.

1923 - Post-war slump in orders experienced by NBL. Atlas Works closed and men laid off.

1931 - Cessation of construction of locomotives by Beardmore & Co.

1933 - Only 16 locomotives built by NBL.

1939 - Boom caused by World War II.

1948 - Atlas Works reopened.

1948 - Formation of British Railways.

1956 - NBL operating at a loss.

1962 - NBL went into receivership. 5,000 jobs lost.

1965 - NBL records donated to the Mitchell Library.

1968 - Cowlairs Works closed, with work transferred to St. Rollox Works.

1970 - St. Rollox Works became part of British Rail Engineering Ltd.

1972 - St. Rollox Works renamed Glasgow Works.

1986 - Springburn Museum opened.

1987 - Glasgow's locomotive industry commemorated by artist George Wyllie's construction and eventual burning of the "Straw Locomotive", with an exhibition in Springburn Museum.

1997 - Springburn Museum's funding reduced by Glasgow City Council.

Bibliography

Much of the information in this book has been obtained from the primary sources retained in the Mitchell Library, Glasgow. These include the company order books, delivery books and other miscellaneous items, and of course the photographs. Many books have been published on railway and locomotive topics, with these containing relevant information on Glasgow built product. The most important published and unpublished material on the story of the locomotive building industry of Glasgow is listed below.

Allchin, M.C.V.
"A History of Highland Locomotives"
Railway Hobbies Ltd., Southsea, 1947, 72pp., ill.

Bradley, Rodger P.
"Giants of Steam: The Full Story of the North British Locomotive Co. Ltd"
Oxford Publishing Co., Sparkford, Somerset, 1995, 192pp., ill.

Clay, John F.
"Jubilees Of The LMS"
Ian Allan, London, 1971, 112pp., bibl., ill.

Cornwell, H.J. Campbell
"Forty Years Of Caledonian Locomotives 1882-1922"
David & Charles, Newton Abbot, 1974, 221pp., bibl, ill.

Highet, Campbell
"Scottish Locomotive History 1831-1923"
George Allen & Unwin Ltd., London, 1970, 240pp., ill., col. ill.

Hume, John R. and Moss, Michael S.
"Beardmore: The History Of A Scottish Industrial Giant"
Heinemann, London, 1979, 364pp., bibl., ill.

Johnston, Ian
"Beardmore Built: The Rise and Fall Of A Clydeside Shipyard"
Clydebank District Libraries & Museums Department, Clydebank, 1993, 192pp., bibl., ill.

Larkin, Edgar
"An Illustrated History Of British Railways' Workshops: Locomotive, Carriage and Wagon Building And Maintenance, From 1825 To The Present Day"
Oxford Publishing Co., Sparkford, Somerset, 1992, 184pp., bibl., ill.

Neilson, Walter Montgomerie
"Dates And Notes Of The Principal Occurrences Of My Life"
Unpublished Manuscript, Glasgow University Archives D10 5/1.

(Nicolson, Murdoch)
"The North British Locomotive Company Collection: A Guide To The Records Of The Company And Its Constituents Held In The Library With A Brief History Of The Companies"
The Mitchell Library, Glasgow, 1974, 23pp., bibl., ill.

Nicolson, Murdoch, and O'Neill, Mark
"Glasgow: Locomotive Builder To The World"
Polygon Books, Edinburgh; Third Eye Centre; Springburn Museum; Glasgow District Libraries
Publications Board, all Glasgow, 1987, 44pp., bibl., ill.

Nock, Oswald S.
"The Royal Scots And Patriots Of The LMS"
David & Charles, Newton Abbot, 1978, 96pp., ill.

Nock, Oswald S.
"The Southern King Arthur Family"
David & Charles, Newton Abbot, 1976, 96pp., ill.

North British Locomotive Company
"A History Of The North British Locomotive Company Ltd"
North British Locomotive Company Ltd., Glasgow, 1953, 115pp., ill., col. ill.

North British Locomotive Company
"An Account Of The Manufacture Of Locomotives And Other Munitions Of War During The
Period Of 1914-1919"
North British Locomotive Company Ltd., Glasgow, 1920, 123pp., ill.

North British Locomotive Company
"North British Locomotives: A Catalogue Of Narrow Gauge Locomotives"
David & Charles, Newton Abbot, 1970, 79pp., ill. Reprint of 1912 edition.

Smith, David L.
"Locomotives Of The Glasgow And South Western Railway"
David & Charles, Newton Abbot, 1976, 192pp., ill.

Stephenson Locomotive Society
"'Little And Good': The Great North of Scotland Railway" Stephenson Locomotive Society,
Newton Hall, Durham, 1972, 112pp., ill.

Thomas, John "The North British Atlantics"
David & Charles, Newton Abbot, 1972, 188pp., ill., col. ill.

Thomas, John
"The Springburn Story: The History Of The Scottish Railway Metropolis"
David & Charles, Dawlish, 1964, 260pp., bibl., ill.